All too often we read quickly through B
the ones we find hard to understand, as i
and Ladders. Michael L. Ruffin helps us t
he takes us through the life of Jesus as tol
itually uplifting experience to read a verse or a couple of verses, to
read them again, and then to be led in prayer over what we have just
read. This book creatively opens a refreshing way to devote ourselves
to prayer as we stroll, as it were, through a Gospel hand-in-hand with
Jesus.

—*David E. Garland*
Professor of Christian Scriptures
George W. Truett Theological Seminary
Baylor University

Praying with Matthew is an excellent addition to your daily devotional
and prayer time. Mike Ruffin's thoughtful and attentive prayers,
combined with selected passages from the Gospel of Matthew, speak
to the depths of the human condition as we seek to communicate
our deepest fears and greatest hopes to God. Mike's many years as a
pastor and professor provide the pastoral context out of which these
prayers emerge. As you pray with Matthew, you will find yourself
immersed in the great story of Scripture and guided by the Spirit as
you seek to incarnate the presence of Jesus in your daily life.

—*Jody Long*
Executive Coordinator
Cooperative Baptist Fellowship of Georgia

Can a few minutes in prayer and Scripture make a difference? Mike
Ruffin answers that question by praying through the Gospel of
Matthew, one snippet of Scripture after another. With his insightful
companionship, we see Scripture with fresh eyes. In a few words of

prayer, we question our ways and look toward the ways God worked long ago. Set a practice to begin the day in this way and see how God is still at work bringing transformation and new life.

—*Cyndi McDonald*
Barnesville First United Methodist Church
Barnesville, Georgia

Insightful. Focused. Clear.

Praying with Matthew offers a trinity of blessings for those of us who relish the daily practice of listening for God. A marvelous way to start—or end—the day!

—*Debra Tregaskis*
Executive Presbyter
Flint River Presbytery

PRAYING WITH MATTHEW

Smyth & Helwys Publishing, Inc.
6316 Peake Road
Macon, Georgia 31210-3960
1-800-747-3016
©2020 by Michael L. Ruffin
All rights reserved.

Library of Congress Cataloging-in-Publication Data

Names: Ruffin, Michael Lee, 1958- author.
Title: Praying with Matthew / by Michael L. Ruffin.
Description: Macon, GA : Smyth & Helwys Publishing, 2020.
Identifiers: LCCN 2020014257 (print) | LCCN 2020014258 (ebook) | ISBN
9781641732505 (paperback) | ISBN 9781641732512 (ebook)
Subjects: LCSH: Bible. Matthew--Devotional literature.
Classification: LCC BS2575.54 .R84 2020 (print) | LCC BS2575.54 (ebook) |
DDC 242/.2--dc23
LC record available at https://lccn.loc.gov/2020014257
LC ebook record available at https://lccn.loc.gov/2020014258

PRAYING WITH
MATTHEW
365 Days of Gospel-Shaped Devotions

MICHAEL L. RUFFIN

ALSO BY MICHAEL L. RUFFIN

Fifty-Seven: A Memoir of Death and Life

The Limp Is Mightier than the Strut and other Sermons

Luke: Parables for the Journey

Prayer 365

Living on the Edge: Preaching Advent in Year C

Why Be a Christian? The Sermons of Howard P. Giddens

Living between the Advents: Preaching Advent in Year B

To my professors in the
Mercer University Department of Christianity (1975–1978)
and at the
Southern Baptist Theological Seminary (1979–1986),
models of scholarly spirituality

ACKNOWLEDGMENTS

The first prayers I ever prayed, as is the case with many children of Christian parents, were the "God is great, God is good, let us thank God for our food" mealtime blessing and the "Now I lay me down to sleep" bedtime prayer. So my parents taught me to pray. They also accidentally taught me the value of the discipline of Scripture-formed prayer. They would sit down every night to read the Scripture passage and related devotion found in their denomination's prayer guide. After they read those words, one of them would offer a spoken prayer. Eventually I was deemed old enough to participate. It was a rite of passage. I am grateful for the model they offered me.

The professors who taught me in the Department of Christianity (now the Department of Religion) at Mercer University and at the Southern Baptist Theological Seminary demonstrated to me and convinced me of the value of diving into the deep places where biblical study and spirituality flow together. I have dedicated this book to all of them, but I'd like to name in particular the late Dr. Robert Otto, who spent decades teaching at Mercer, and to Dr. Glenn Hinson, who taught at Southern for thirty years, including the time I was there, and later at other schools including the Baptist Theological Seminary at Richmond and the Baptist Seminary of Kentucky. Their spiritual scholarship (or scholarly spirituality) left an indelible impression on me.

The people in the churches I served as pastor over the years helped inspire my commitment to developing a life of prayer. I am grateful to have prayed with and for them.

Counting from the Friday night in the fall of 1976 that we prayed over the dinner we were about to eat on our first date, my wife Debra and I have been praying together for forty-four years. I pray we get to continue doing so for many years to come.

INTRODUCTION

Communication with God is basic to the Christian life. We communicate with God in many ways. One way is through prayer. Another is through listening to Scripture. A third is through communing with the Holy Spirit.

As you use this book, I hope you find that it brings together those three ways of communicating with God. I think that's what happened in the writing of the prayers contained in it. Every morning over the course of a year, I read a portion of the Gospel of Matthew. As I prayed and communed with the Spirit, I listened for the word of God. I then wrote a prayer based on that experience.

Now you bring your own life to this process. As you read the Gospel of Matthew and read my prayers, I hope you will enter into prayer, into reverent listening for the word of the Lord, and into communion with the Spirit. I hope you will pray your own prayers. I hope this book contributes to your communication with God.

The book's layout is simple. It is divided into 365 days. For each day, I've provided a reading from the Gospel of Matthew and a prayer. I encourage you to reflect on the Gospel reading before reading the prayer. It might prove worthwhile to then reread the Matthew passage in light of the prayer.

As you read, you will notice that some devotions consist of only a prayer, but others first offer some comments on that day's Matthew reading. To my way of thinking, the comments are part of my communication with God. In this work, and at all times, I try to offer up my thought processes to God in prayer. But it seemed wise to differentiate between the comments and the prayers, so in those devotions that contain both, a blank line separates them.

I pray that God will use this book to help you grow in your life of prayer and in your relationship with God.

DAY 1: HERITAGE

The record of the genealogy of Jesus the Messiah, the son of David, the son of Abraham. (Matthew 1:1, NASB)

O God,

Everyone has a heritage; everyone has the facts, legends, histories, experiences, reflections, and DNA that have been handed down to us by the generations that preceded us.

There are aspects of our heritage for which we praise you always; there are aspects of our heritage for which we praise you anyhow.

Lord, help us embrace our heritage that we might both live up to it and live beyond it.

Thank you for those who came before us to pave the way for us. Thank you for your grace that enabled them to be. Thank you for your grace that empowered them to be part of your purpose.

Jesus had a heritage and so do we. Lead us to learn from both his heritage and ours of the power of your grace.

Amen.

DAY 2: BY GRACE THROUGH FAITH

Judah was the father of Perez and Zerah by Tamar . . . Salmon was the father of Boaz by Rahab, Boaz was the father of Obed by Ruth . . . and David was the father of Solomon by Bathsheba who had been the wife of Uriah. (Matthew 1:3, 5-6, NASB)

Matthew's genealogy of Jesus is remarkable in that it includes the names of some of the women who were in Jesus' family tree and in that all the women it names became branches on that tree in rather interesting ways.

Indeed, those women were people over whom some—maybe many—in their day would have stood in judgment and over whom some—maybe many—in our day would stand in judgment.

One could say the same thing about many—if not most or even all—of the men in the tree as well.

And one could say the same thing about all of us who have been grafted onto Jesus' family tree.

Thank you, God, for your grace; thank you, God, for our faith.

Thank you that, while sanctification is our goal, perfection is not required.

Thank you for the remarkable ways in which you include even us in your story of salvation.

Help us not to stand in judgment over others or over ourselves. Help us, rather, to celebrate the working of your amazing grace in us all.

Amen.

DAY 3: GOD'S PURPOSES

So all the generations from Abraham to David are fourteen generations; from David to the deportation to Babylon, fourteen generations; and from the deportation to Babylon to the Messiah, fourteen generations. (Matthew 1:17, NASB)

O God,

Sometimes we err in not making the effort to consider the ways in which it all fits together, in which case we are not attentive enough to your purposes.

Sometimes we err in making too much of an effort to make it all fit together, in which case we reduce your purposes to what we can comprehend.

Perhaps the best thing we can do, O God, is to trust that you are working your purposes out and to live humbly with the best understanding of them that we can achieve—an understanding that grows all the time.

Help us so to trust, O God, and to base our understanding on the truth that Jesus Christ is the centerpiece and thus the heart and soul of what your purposes are all about.

Amen.

DAY 4: FOUND TO BE

Now the birth of Jesus the Messiah took place in this way. When his mother Mary had been engaged to Joseph, but before they lived together, she was found to be with child from the Holy Spirit. (Matthew 1:18, NRSV)

Perhaps we should not be surprised when God chooses to come to us. Perhaps we should expect for Christ to come to make his home in us.

Perhaps, though, we should be ready to be surprised at the ways God chooses to come to us; perhaps we should expect to be shocked and overwhelmed at the ways in which Christ comes to make his home in us.

Forgive us, Lord, for our failure to expect your coming to us. Lead us always to be on the lookout for your coming.

Forgive us, Lord, for our arrogant assumptions about how you will or even must come to us. Lead us always to be open to your surprising and even shocking ways of approaching and entering our lives.

If we look, we will find you. If we look from a different angle, we may find you in a different way.

Amaze us, O God—and make us ready to be amazed.

Amen.

DAY 5: RIGHTEOUS

Her husband Joseph, being a righteous man and unwilling to expose her to public disgrace, planned to dismiss her quietly. (Matthew 1:19, NRSV)

Lord, protect us from the posturing, preening, and publicity seeking that accompany the "righteousness" that we bestow on ourselves. Indeed, protect us from any thinking or acting that would attempt to correlate righteousness with personal goodness or with personal gain.

Instead, Lord, give us real righteousness—the righteousness that causes us to want to do right by you by doing right by other people. May our righteousness—our right relationship with you, which is a gift of your grace—show itself in the ways that we treat people who are in trouble, who are in pain, who are in shame, or who are in a predicament.

Help us, Lord, to care about how it is and how it looks for other people more than we care about how it is and how it looks for us.

Amen.

DAY 6: DON'T BE AFRAID

But just when he had resolved to do this, an angel of the Lord appeared to him in a dream and said, 'Joseph, son of David, do not be afraid to take Mary as your wife, for the child conceived in her is from the Holy Spirit. (Matthew 1:20, NRSV)

O God, when you communicate your will and way to us—whether it be through the living of our lives, through the thinking of our thoughts, through the dreaming of our dreams, or through the praying of our prayers—help us not to be afraid.

When you communicate your will and way to us through your messenger—whether it be through your Spirit, through your proclaimers, through your Book, or through your creation—help us not to be afraid.

After all, why should we be afraid? Should we be afraid of your communication to us of your will and way just because you turn our world upside down, just because you reverse our preconceived notions, just because you challenge our sense of right and wrong, and just because you call us to sacrifice our pride?

O God, even as we ask you to communicate your will and way to us and to empower us to be open to them, we beg you . . . help us not to be afraid.

Amen.

DAY 7: SAVE

She will bear a son, and you are to name him Jesus, for he will save his people from their sins. (Matthew 1:21, NRSV)

Lord, help us admit that we are lost and that, left on our own, we will remain lost; help us admit that even after we are saved from our lostness, we tend to wander off on our own and get ourselves in trouble.

Help us acknowledge our sins, particularly the primary sin that causes us to try to be our own god and to try to find our own way, attempts that lead us to the secondary sins that are symptomatic of the primary one.

Show us the basic and simple wisdom of trusting you, depending on you, and following you for the sake of our life here and for the sake of our life in the hereafter.

Thank you for your Son Jesus, whose name means "Salvation" and in whom you graciously provide a way for us to trust in you daringly, to depend on you fully, and to follow you recklessly.

Amen.

DAY 8: GOD IS WITH US

All this took place to fulfill what had been spoken by the Lord through the prophet: "Look, the virgin shall conceive and bear a son, and they shall name him Emmanuel," which means, "God is with us." (Matthew 1:22-23, NRSV)

We have difficulty comprehending the fact that the spiritual is as real as the physical; it is part of the price we pay for being human, for experiencing and knowing nothing apart from these bodies of ours.

And so, O God, in Jesus Christ, in the baby born to the Virgin Mary, you came to us in and as a physical human being to concretize and enflesh for a little while the perpetual spiritual reality that is so hard for us to get our minds around, namely, that you are with us.

Thank you, God, for going so far to enable us to be better able to comprehend the truth of your grace: God is with us.

Enable us to live in perpetual awareness of and in perpetual celebration of that perpetual reality.

Amen.

DAY 9: AS COMMANDED

When Joseph awoke from sleep, he did as the angel of the Lord commanded him; he took her as his wife, but had no marital relations with her until she had borne a son; and he named him Jesus. (Matthew 1:24-25, NRSV)

We tend to read or look right past those places in the Bible, in history, in literature, or in the lives of people around us where somebody does as the Lord commands them.

We should not, because there are important lessons to be learned from such amazing acts.

O Lord, help us pay closer attention so we can learn appropriately about obedience.

Give us courage to do what you command or lead us to do, regardless of how it might run against the grain of our preferences or the expectations of our culture—which it almost certainly will do.

Give us grace to accept adjustments to the ways we act and even to the ways we think, feel, and desire, if such adjustments are necessary to our obedience—which they almost certainly will be.

Give us humility to understand that our obedience, while it will do us good, is not finally for our personal good but rather for the good of your purposes and your kingdom, regardless of how hard such humility is to achieve—which it almost certainly will be.

Help us want to do what you command us. Then help us do it. Amen.

DAY 10: WISDOM

After Jesus was born in Bethlehem in the territory of Judea during the rule of King Herod, magi came from the east to Jerusalem. (Matthew 2:1, CEB)

The wise men were wise to go all that way and to all that trouble to see Jesus, weren't they?

If you want to see him in this time and place, all you have to do is turn your eyes and your heart a little bit and he's right there. Odd as it seems, though, doing that seems to be harder than what the wise men had to do.

God, give us
the desire to see Jesus,
the drive to see Jesus, and
the desperation to see Jesus
that will turn our eyes and our hearts—that will turn our lives—to him.
Amen.

DAY 11: CURIOSITY

They asked, "Where is the newborn king of the Jews? We've seen his star in the east, and we've come to honor him." (Matthew 2:2, CEB)

It's safe to say that, whether or not the wise men were professional astronomers, they observed the star that signaled Jesus' birth because they were looking for . . . something.

It's also safe to say that those who were looking for nothing saw that, too.

Give us, O God, a great curiosity for what you might be up to—in this universe, in this world, in this neighborhood, and in these lives— that causes us always to be on the lookout for what you are up to, and that then compels us to follow up on what we see you being up to—just so we can see what you will be up to next.

Amen.

DAY 12: INQUIRY

He gathered all the chief priests and the legal experts and asked them where the Christ was to be born. (Matthew 2:4, CEB)

Herod was motivated by fear to inquire into the birthplace of the Messiah. He was looking for information he could use to protect his place and his standing—to protect himself. Herod wanted to learn about Jesus so he could manage and control Jesus, which for him meant to eliminate Jesus from his life.

O God, help our inquiries into Jesus not to be motivated by fear.

While we would never think of using what we can find out about Jesus to try to eliminate him from our lives, the truth is that if we are driven by fear to learn of him, we will be looking only for those aspects of him that we think either eliminate or confirm our fear.

Either way, we will delude ourselves into thinking that we have managed and controlled him, that we have used him for what we need, and that we have no further need for him. We will thereby not have eliminated him from our lives, but we will have tried to relegate him to only those areas of our lives where we think we need him.

O God, help our inquiries into Jesus be motivated by a desire to know his grace and love in every aspect and area of our lives, and by a desire to submit ourselves to him in every aspect and area of our lives.

Herod saw Jesus as a problem to be confirmed and eliminated. Help us not to see him only as a way to confirm or to eliminate our problems but rather to see him as what he is: the Messiah and Savior who would be and should be Lord of our whole lives.

Amen.

DAY 13: INSIGNIFICANCE

They said, "In Bethlehem of Judea, for this is what the prophet wrote: You, Bethlehem, land of Judah, by no means are you least among the rulers of Judah, because from you will come one who governs, who will shepherd my people Israel." (Matthew 2:5-6, CEB)

Sometimes we underestimate ourselves. Sometimes we might be surprised at just what can come out of us.

God, help us look for what you want to accomplish in and through us.

Cause us to see that, regardless of how insignificant we think we are, you might have plans to do something significant through us.

Enable us also to see that, if something appears insignificant to the world and even to us, it is significant if you are behind it and in it.

May we want nothing more or less than to be useful in what you are up to in bringing your grace to bear on the world.

Amen.

DAY 14: SECOND-HAND NEWS AND FALSE PRETENSES

Then Herod secretly called for the magi and found out from them the time when the star had first appeared. He sent them to Bethlehem, saying, "Go and search carefully for the child. When you've found him, report to me so that I too may go and honor him." (Matthew 2:7-8, CEB)

There were at least two things wrong with Herod's request of the wise men.

In the first place, Herod was willing to accept the expertise, witness, and testimony of the wise men rather than going to find out about Jesus for himself.

In the second place, Herod's quest by proxy was based on false pretenses; he wanted Jesus found not so he could worship him but rather so he could contain and even eliminate Jesus from his life.

God, we all are, whether we know it or not and whether we acknowledge it or not, seeking Jesus. May our quest be a willing one that is pursued with integrity and with the best motives we can muster.

While we admit our need for and humbly accept the guidance of those who have gone before us, don't let us accept the testimony of others about Jesus. Compel us rather to seek him, to find him, to experience him, and to know him for ourselves.

Inspire us to seek Jesus with honest motives. Help us seek life in his huge world rather than trying to fit him into our little worlds. Help us submit ourselves to the wonder and grace of all that he is instead of trying to find out just enough about him to let ourselves think we can manage or manipulate him.

Help us, God, to seek Jesus for ourselves and to do so with honesty and openness.

Amen.

DAY 15: OVERWHELMED

When they heard the king, they went; and look, the star they had seen in the east went ahead of them until it stood over the place where the child was. When they saw the star, they were filled with joy. (Matthew 2:9-10, CEB)

We are all on a pilgrimage. We are all on a journey. Whether we know it or not and whether we acknowledge it or not, Jesus Christ is the goal of the pilgrimage and the journey.

There will come a day—thank you, God—when we will know Jesus Christ fully and freely. We look forward to reaching that ultimate goal. We anticipate the great joy that will accompany it.

It is the case, though, that we know Jesus and are known by him, and that we love Jesus and are loved by him, in every moment all along the way. Help us acknowledge and appreciate the joy that is ours in the experience of such knowledge and love, both in the routine and in the ordinary.

Forgive us for our immaturity that causes us to hold out for the joy that accompanies the spectacular.

On the other hand, forgive our inattention that causes us to miss the spectacular and the joy that accompanies it.

Cause us to be overwhelmed with joy over Jesus, both in the realm of the routine and in the realm of the spectacular.

Amen.

DAY 16: GIFTS

They entered the house and saw the child with Mary his mother. Falling to their knees, they honored him. Then they opened their treasure chests and presented him with gifts of gold, frankincense, and myrrh. (Matthew 2:11, CEB)

How can we not want to give the best we have to the One that we regard as King, Lord, and Savior?

How can we not want to respond to his love and sacrifice with our love and sacrifice?

O God, we know so much more about the kind of king Jesus is than did those wise men who brought him their gifts when he was so small, when he was so far away from his cross and his empty tomb. We know that he was a king who would reign through love, grace, service, and sacrifice; that he was a king who would ascend to his throne only after he had given himself completely away.

Help us, O God, through the power of your grace and through the strength of your Holy Spirit, to love, to give, to serve, and to sacrifice in ways that befit the servants of such a King.

Amen.

DAY 17: BY ANOTHER ROAD

Because they were warned in a dream not to return to Herod, they went back to their own country by another route. (Matthew 2:12, CEB)

We're all heading somewhere in these lives of ours, and, truth be told, there are probably many different roads that will get us there. And maybe there is more than one somewhere that would be appropriate for each of us.

The thing is that we have no way of knowing what lies down a particular road. It stands to reason that, life being what life is, no road is without its dangers, rewards, promises, and disappointments.

That doesn't mean, though, that we should be careless about which road we choose. Indeed, we should follow the best light we have and choose the best road we can. After all, not all roads are equal. Some roads are better than others.

Lord, help us follow the guidance that you make available to us, be it through thoughts, through dreams, through Scripture, through your Spirit, through friends, or through other means.

May the roads we choose be ones that will lead us to do no harm to others but rather to do good to others. May the roads we choose not only get us where we are headed but also get us there along the path that will enable us to be the most productive that we can be—to do the most good for you and for others.

Amen.

DAY 18: FLEE

When the magi had departed, an angel from the Lord appeared to Joseph in a dream and said, "Get up. Take the child and his mother and escape to Egypt. Stay there until I tell you, for Herod will soon search for the child in order to kill him." (Matthew 2:13, CEB)

It is strange and sad but nonetheless true: whereas home should be the place where you find safety, sometimes you have to flee to another place—even a strange and foreign place—to find it.

It is strange and sad but nonetheless true: sometimes our own family or our own community family or our own faith family can prove dangerous or manipulative or even abusive, and when that happens, we have to flee. We have to find shelter and protection where we can.

O Lord, help us be the kinds of families at home or in our communities or in our churches that provide affirmation, nurture, growth, protection, and safety to all our family members. Help us foster an atmosphere and a reality in which the members of our family can live, love, thrive, and be safe.

O Lord, forgive us when we, by our actions or our inactions or by our feelings or our lack of feelings, make our home feel unsafe, insecure, or unhealthy for anyone.

And, O Lord, when it is best that we flee, help us do so with great faith and boldness, ready to find safety and protection in the most surprising places and in the most surprising people.

Amen.

DAY 19: OUT OF EGYPT

Joseph got up and, during the night, took the child and his mother to Egypt. He stayed there until Herod died. This fulfilled what the Lord had spoken through the prophet: I have called my son out of Egypt. (Matthew 2:14-15, CEB)

Biblically speaking, God calling God's son out of Egypt is a big deal.

First it was God's child Israel that God called out of Egypt, where they had gone due to the leadership of a man named Joseph.

Then it was God's child Jesus that God called out of Egypt, where he had gone due to the leadership of another man named Joseph.

In both cases it was an exodus out of a strange land that had offered temporary sanctuary during threatening times and into a land where the kingdom of God would be announced and established. Frankly, the land to which they were going turned out to be more hazardous than the one they left, but it was in the long run worth it because they were doing the work of the kingdom of God.

Help us, Lord, to come out of Egypt. Help us to forsake the seeming shelter and security of locations and situations outside the risky and hazardous kingdom of God, that realm where we are called—expected, even—to lose our lives and to give ourselves away for the sake of that kingdom.

Remind us that it is in the long run worth it because we are, after all, doing the work of the kingdom of God.

Amen.

DAY 20: KNOWLEDGE

When Herod knew the magi had fooled him, he grew very angry. He sent soldiers to kill all the children in Bethlehem and in all the surrounding territory who were two years old and younger, according to the time that he had learned from the magi. (Matthew 2:16, CEB)

Knowledge is value neutral; how we choose to use knowledge is not.

The wise men and Herod had the same knowledge concerning the general time frame within which Jesus was born, although the wise men had it first and then shared it with Herod.

The wise men used their knowledge to find Jesus and worship him. Herod used that same knowledge to try to find Jesus and kill him.

Some use their knowledge about germs to wage war against disease. Others use their knowledge about germs to develop germ-based weapons for people to use in waging war against each other.

Some use their knowledge of nuclear physics to make advances in the production of energy. Others use their knowledge of nuclear physics to make advances in the production of bombs.

Some use their knowledge of information technology to enhance the flow of information. Others use their knowledge of information technology to increase the flow of disinformation.

O God, inspire us to use our knowledge for good and not for evil, for help and not for harm, for building up and not for tearing down, and for love and not for hate.

May we apply our knowledge graciously and ethically. May we always be thinking about how you would have us use it and about how we can do the most good with it.

Amen.

DAY 21: RACHEL'S WEEPING

A voice was heard in Ramah, weeping and much grieving. Rachel weeping for her children, and she did not want to be comforted, because they were no more. (Matthew 2:18, CEB)

When the prophet Jeremiah spoke these words some six centuries before Matthew's Gospel was produced, he was talking about something that had happened in the not-too-distant past, namely, the carrying off of Israelites by the Assyrians in the late eighth century BCE, a deportation for which Ramah was a departure point. "Rachel" in that case wept because her children—the Joseph tribes—had experienced the deaths or deportations of most of their members.

Matthew picked up Jeremiah's words and used them to try to bring some meaning to what has come to be known as the "Slaughter of the Innocents" by Herod's armies in his simultaneously crazed and calculated effort to kill the infant Jesus. Perhaps Matthew was attracted to the text by the tradition that Rachel's burial place was near Bethlehem.

Regardless, Matthew's use of Jeremiah's words, even though he took them out of their historical context, is appropriate, since the Bethlehem tragedy certainly elicited the same kind of grief as the one referenced by Jeremiah. It was the same kind of tragedy: the destruction of people, of family, and of tribal and national bonds by people whose cruelty was fueled by their quest to preserve and extend their power.

O God, It is a terrible sadness that the destruction of children and other innocent people and the destruction of family, tribal, and national bonds still happens in this "civilized" world of ours because of the crazed, cruel, and calculated actions of people who are intent on preserving and expanding their power—and because of the apathy of good people who let them get away with it.

We still hear Rachel weeping.

Forgive us, Lord—and lead us to do something about it.

Amen.

DAY 22: SAFE

After King Herod died, an angel from the Lord appeared in a dream to Joseph in Egypt. "Get up," the angel said, "and take the child and his mother and go to the land of Israel. Those who were trying to kill the child are dead." Joseph got up, took the child and his mother, and went to the land of Israel. But when he heard that Archelaus ruled over Judea in place of his father Herod, Joseph was afraid to go there. (Matthew 2:19-22a, CEB)

On one hand, it was safe for Joseph to take his family back to Israel. On the other hand, it wasn't.

It is the way of the world and it is the way of faithful pilgrimage that when one danger is eliminated or lessened, another one rises or increases in its place.

Jesus was always safe but he was never safe, and Jesus was never safe but he was always safe. It was that way all through his life—it was even that way as he hung on the cross. Even as he suffered and died, he was safe in the love and will of the Father; even as he was safe in the love and will of the Father, he suffered and died.

O God, help us rest safe in your love and will, even as we live boldly in the dangers and threats that confront use. Help us live boldly in the dangers and threats that confront us, even as we rest safe in your love and will.

That was your way for your Son who is our Teacher and Lord. It is right that your way for him be your way for us, his apprentices and followers.

Help us submit to it.

Amen.

DAY 23: REPENT

In those days John the Baptist appeared in the wilderness of Judea, proclaiming, "Repent, for the kingdom of heaven has come near." (Matthew 3:1-2, NRSV)

John the Baptist, whose preaching was meant to prepare people for the coming of the Messiah, told people that the best way to prepare was to repent, which means to turn around and go the other way. They should do so, he told them, because the kingdom of heaven had come near, by which he meant that the rule of God was about to break into the world in a unique way.

O God, help us listen to John, to your other messengers, to your Holy Spirit, and to your Book, all of which continue to call us to turn from our self-centered and self-defeating ways and to turn toward you so that we can spend the rest of our lives going toward you until finally, one day, we get there.

Give us eyes to see, ears to hear, minds to perceive, and spirits to believe that in Jesus, the reign of God did come and does continue. May our turning lead us to follow him ever more closely as we walk the road on which you lead us.

Amen.

DAY 24: THE WILDERNESS

This is the one of whom the prophet Isaiah spoke when he said, "The voice of one crying out in the wilderness: 'Prepare the way of the Lord, make his paths straight.'" (Matthew 3:3, NRSV)

When the prophet of the Babylonian exile whose words are found in Isaiah 40 spoke the words cited here by Matthew, he was calling the people in exile to herald the impending advent of the Lord, who would cross the wilderness between Israel and Babylon in order to take the

Lord's people home. "Make things ready, make your lives ready," the prophet said, "because the Lord is coming to take you home!"

John the Baptist cried out in the wilderness; it was the wilderness of Judea in which he preached, but he was still heralding the coming of the Lord, still imploring people to make their lives ready for the Lord who would come to make a home with them.

O God, we praise you that in Jesus Christ your Son, you came to make your home with us. We praise you that in Jesus Christ your Son, you came to enable us to make our home with you.

O God, forgive us for our willingness to live as if we are still on the far side of the wilderness, to live as if you have not crossed that wilderness to enable us to live in communion with you.

O God, help us in the ways we act, talk, think, and feel always to be aware of and to respond to your grace so that in, with, and through you, we always keep the way prepared and the paths straight.

Amen.

DAY 25: LEGITIMATE AND AUTHENTIC

Now John wore clothing of camel's hair with a leather belt around his waist, and his food was locusts and wild honey. (Matthew 3:4, NRSV)

Matthew is doing more here than telling us that John the Baptist was an interesting-looking and interesting character, although John certainly was that. Through his physical description of John, Matthew is communicating to us that John followed in the tradition of the great biblical prophets who had come before him, especially the prophet Elijah.

It is good for all of us to remember the long line at the end of which we stand. There have been many people who have gone before us who have done a lot of faithful thinking, praying, talking, and living. Our faith and practice are but the latest word in a long book God has been writing through God's people for countless generations.

John could not have been aware of every person, every belief, and every word that had preceded him, and neither can we. We can, though, be as aware as humanly possible of who and what has come before us, and we can exercise appropriate humility and gratitude for those who passed along a framework within which we can express our faith.

Lord, thank you for those who have gone before us. Forgive us for the arrogance we sometimes exhibit in the ways we claim ownership of our faith as if it somehow started with us. Forgive us as well for the carelessness we sometimes exhibit in the ways that we fail to rethink and reframe our inherited traditions for our own time and context.

Help us be enough like those who have gone before us to be legitimate and enough unlike them to be authentic.

Amen.

DAY 26: BAPTISM AND CONFESSION

Then the people of Jerusalem and all Judea were going out to him, and all the region along the Jordan, and they were baptized by him in the river Jordan, confessing their sins. (Matthew 3:5-6, NRSV)

The two things look to be so closely related that we can see them as being of one piece: the people were baptized, which meant they were confessing their sins; they confessed their sins, which meant they were baptized.

Lord, some of us have not been baptized, but we will be. When we are, give us grace to confess our sins, and give us grace to know that in confessing them and in being swept by the water into your kingdom, we find forgiveness and well-being.

Lord, some of us have been baptized, but we need to recall and to relive the experience. When we do, give us grace to remember that we in our baptism confessed our sins and found forgiveness and well-being, and give us grace to know that we still need to turn toward you in confession and for forgiveness and well-being.

Baptism is confession; confession is baptism. May the honest confession and the humble admission that accompanies baptism always characterize our living.

Amen.

DAY 27: BROOD OF VIPERS

But when he saw many Pharisees and Sadducees coming for baptism, he said to them, "You brood of vipers! Who warned you to flee from the wrath to come?" (Matthew 3:7, NRSV)

What did John sense about or know about or suspect about those people who were so serious about their religion that he would say such a thing to them as they were coming to him for baptism?

Was it that they were insincere? Was it that they were doing it for show? Was it that they were caught up in the emotion of the moment? Was it that they had a sense of entitlement? Was it that they saw no need to change and had no intention of changing?

Was it that they were so serious about their religion?

Whatever it was about them that caused John to say that terrible thing, O God, protect us from it. Whatever it was, O God, drive it from us. Whatever it was, O God, if it is in us, enable us by your grace to turn away from it and to you.

If such words apply to us, O God, help us hear them.

Then give us honest, aware, humble, and repentant hearts.

Amen.

DAY 28: GOOD FRUIT

> *"Bear fruit worthy of repentance. Do not presume to say
> to yourselves, 'We have Abraham as our ancestor'; for I
> tell you, God is able from these stones to raise up chil-
> dren to Abraham. Even now the ax is lying at the root
> of the trees; every tree therefore that does not bear good
> fruit is cut down and thrown into the fire." (Matthew
> 3:8-10, NRSV)*

It is not enough to come from good stock, to have a good pedigree, or
to have an impressive family tree. Guard us, O Lord, from the presumption or the carelessness that would let us think so.

Help us rather to repent. Help us find the way that we should
go by intentionally turning away from our doomed-to-fail efforts at
self-determination and turning instead toward a bound-to-succeed
commitment to your direction.

Then we will bear the fruit that is worthy of repentance, fruit
that has labels such as "humble" and "grateful" and "receptive" and
"trusting." Such fruit remains fresh and survives; not so with the rotting
fruit that labels such as "proud" and "entitled" and "self-reliant" and
"self-centered."

Help us bear good fruit, O Lord.
Amen.

DAY 29: THE HOLY SPIRIT
AND FIRE

> *"I baptize you with water for repentance, but one who
> is more powerful than I is coming after me; I am not
> worthy to carry his sandals. He will baptize you with the
> Holy Spirit and fire. His winnowing fork is in his hand,
> and he will clear his threshing floor and will gather his*

wheat into the granary; but the chaff he will burn with unquenchable fire." (Matthew 3:11-12, NRSV)

We thank you, O God, for the assurance that evaluation, judgment, and justice are in the hands of the Son of God, and not in the hands of beings who are as frail and fallible as we are, even ones as spectacularly in touch with you as people like John the Baptist were and are. We trust that the separation of the wheat from the chaff is and will be conducted according to your justice, love, mercy, and grace.

We are all of mixed character and quality, aren't we? We all need our chaff to be separated from our wheat, don't we?

So we thank you, O God, for the Spirit with which Jesus touches us and through which he shows us how to be his disciples, affirms us when we are heading in the right direction, and convicts us when we are not.

We thank you, O God, for the fire with which Jesus touches us and through which he takes away and destroys that which hinders our discipleship to him and our relationship with you.

Make us bold to embrace the work of the Spirit and of the fire in our lives.

Amen.

DAY 30: JESUS . . . CAME TO BE BAPTIZED

Then Jesus came from Galilee to John at the Jordan, to be baptized by him. (Matthew 3:13, NRSV)

It was another step in the series of humble—even humiliating—steps that Jesus made. The series began with the Incarnation and ended with the Crucifixion, and along the way there were many other similar, if not quite as dramatic or extreme, steps.

And so he who knew no sin, he who had no need to repent, came to John at the Jordan River so that he could get in line with all the other people who had come, so he could get wet with all the other people who had come, so he could submit to what God was doing through John with all the other people who had come—so he could be baptized with all the other people who had come.

Thank you, God, that Jesus humbled himself through baptism and in so many other ways.

Thank you, God, that Jesus joined himself to our condition and identified himself with our sinful state through his baptism and in so many other ways—especially through his death on the cross.

Help us, O God, to live baptized lives that show our identification with Jesus in his humility.

Amen.

DAY 31: DO YOU COME TO ME?

John would have prevented him, saying, "I need to be baptized by you, and do you come to me?" But Jesus answered him, "Let it be so now; for it is proper for us in this way to fulfill all righteousness." Then he consented. (Matthew 3:14-15, NRSV)

John the Baptist appropriately recognized when Jesus came to him for baptism that, in light of who he was and in light of who Jesus was, he needed to be baptized by Jesus. But Jesus wanted John to recognize that the submission of Jesus to God's will for him and his willing identification with sinful humanity necessarily preceded the submission of sinners to him and the identification of sinners with him.

Before John or anyone else could—and can—submit to and identify with Jesus, they had—and have—to accept the fact that Jesus first submitted himself to God and first identified himself with them.

We have to receive who Jesus is and what he has done before we can give ourselves to him. We have to see that he has come to us before we can come to him.

Help us, O Lord, willingly to receive the grace that compels Jesus to come to us.

Help us, O Lord, willingly to respond to that grace with our lives. Amen.

DAY 32: OPENED HEAVENS

And when Jesus had been baptized, just as he came up from the water, suddenly the heavens were opened to him and he saw the Spirit of God descending like a dove and alighting on him. (Matthew 3:16, NRSV)

Jesus' baptism somehow prompted an amazing representation of the thing that Jesus' life in its entirety was about: the barrier between heaven and earth was penetrated and the way from heaven to earth and from earth to heaven was opened.

Perhaps when we are baptized, when we enter into the thing that Jesus' life was about, we have a similar experience.

O God, we praise you because in Jesus you brought heaven to earth and made it possible for earth to experience heaven.

O God, increase our awareness—or maybe begin our awareness—of the way in which the heavens have been opened to us through Jesus Christ our Lord.

Make us so heavenly minded that we will be good for something on earth.

Amen.

DAY 33: THE BELOVED

And a voice from heaven said, "This is my Son, the beloved, with whom I am well pleased." (Matthew 3:17, NRSV)

The voice of the Father said that Jesus was the Father's beloved Son before Jesus had done anything, as far as we know from the record at least, to earn the Father's blessing of love.

That is precisely the point: the Father's blessing of love is not and cannot be earned. The Father loved Jesus just because Jesus was Jesus, and the Father loves me just because I am me, and the Father loves you just because you are you.

The Father loves us because we are the Father's children.

Help us know, Father, that you love us.
Help us rest, Father, in your love for us.
Help us hear you say, Father, that you are well pleased with us.
Then help us, Father, live our lives in light of your love, your blessing, and your pleasure.
Amen.

DAY 34: LED . . . TO BE TEMPTED

Then the Spirit led Jesus up into the wilderness so that the devil might tempt him. (Matthew 4:1, CEB)

It's an interesting juxtaposition: the Spirit led Jesus into the wilderness; in the wilderness, the devil tempted Jesus. It's not hard to conclude that the Spirit led Jesus to the place where he would face temptations because somehow the temptations offered by the devil were necessary to Jesus' development and maturation.

It's also not hard to conclude that if that's the way it was for Jesus, it just might be that way for us.

O God, lead us not to places in our lives that harbor temptation for us.

But if you must lead us to such places, whether they be outside or inside us, help us to deal with our temptations in a way that will be for our ultimate benefit and will help lead to the clarification of our identity as your children and as Jesus' followers.

If and when we must face the devil, remind us that we are empowered to face him by your Spirit. You care enough about our growth and progress to lead us to face the devil if that is what we need to do, and you would not lead us into such a battle without also giving us the resources to win it.

Amen.

DAY 35: FAMISHED

After Jesus had fasted for forty days and forty nights, he was starving. (Matthew 4:2, CEB)

It's a vivid picture of Jesus' humanity: he so badly needed and wanted communion with his Father that he was willing to pay any price for it and to go through any suffering to have it.

God, fill us with such a desire to know you and to commune with you that we will give up whatever we have to give up and do whatever we have to do in order to focus all the energies of our spirit on you.

God, form in us a spirit that is willing to forego even what we think we need in order to gain what we need.

Amen.

DAY 36: BY EVERY WORD

The tempter came to him and said, "Since you are God's Son, command these stones to become bread." Jesus replied, "It's written, People won't live only by bread, but by every word spoken by God." (Matthew 4:3-4, CEB)

Jesus was famished after his forty days of fasting, and he had it in his power to turn stones into bread. It's hard to imagine that, under the same circumstances, any one of us would not have done what the tempter suggested. Jesus, though, kept the big picture and the larger good in mind; while not denying that people need bread to survive, he affirmed that we need the spiritual sustenance that comes only from God to be truly alive.

Jesus would not trade the eternally good for the temporarily helpful.

Lord God, we cannot deny our physical needs and appetites, but forgive us for the times when we think primarily of them or even only of them.

Develop in us the kind of life that craves spiritual sustenance even more than it craves physical sustenance.

Help us have the kind of discipline that goes without a physical need for a set time in order to help us become more aware of our spiritual needs and of the resources that you have to meet those needs. Make us aware that, at the end of such a set time of fasting, the temptation to fall back into reliance on the same old patterns will be great; give us strength at such times to turn even more fully to you.

Amen.

DAY 37: ON THE PINNACLE

After that the devil brought him into the holy city and stood him at the highest point of the temple . . . . (Matthew 4:5, CEB)

There may be no more dangerous place to be than on the pinnacle, than on a high place, than at the peak—the view from there can get mighty skewed.

We might get impressed with ourselves for having gotten ourselves there.

Or we might have sold our souls to the devil to get there.

Jesus knew it was the devil that got him there this time. Jesus also knew there was another way for him to get to another pinnacle; it was a much harder way, but it was the right way because it was God's way, and so it was a much better pinnacle.

And so when he looked around and saw the entire world beneath him—and the devil beside him—he was not impressed.

God, if we are to have success, if we are to find ourselves on the pinnacle, let it be because we have lived life the way you called Jesus to live his. Let it be because, overwhelmed by your love and driven by your grace, we gave and gave and gave ourselves away until we had no more to give.

Don't let it be because we let ourselves see things from the devil's perspective.

Amen.

DAY 38: PRESUMPTION

He said to him, "Since you are God's Son, throw yourself down; for it is written, I will command my angels concerning you, and they will take you up in their hands so that you won't hit your foot on a stone." Jesus replied, "Again it's written, Don't test the Lord your God." (Matthew 4:6-7, CEB)

Jesus could have utter trust that if he fell into danger in the course of living his life and fulfilling his calling, the angels of the Lord would take care of him in whatever way he needed to be cared for, whether or not it meant physical rescue.

That's faith—and we can have it too.

But Jesus would not presume upon the favor of God by intentionally doing things that were outside the flow of his faithful life or outside the parameters of his faithful service, thereby daring God to take care of him anyway.

That's presumption—and we don't need it, either.

As Jesus knew and as Jesus found, there is danger aplenty in just being and doing what God has made us and called us to be and do.

If Jesus had thrown himself down from the pinnacle of the temple that day, maybe the angels would have saved him from getting hurt. Jesus would have had his life saved—but what would he have lost in the process?

This much we know: when the time came for Jesus to be lifted up on the cross, and he no doubt desperately wanted to cry out for the angels to take him down and to stop him from being hurt, he didn't do it.

And so he lost his life. But think of what he—and we—gained.

Help us, O Lord, to submit in trust to your tender mercies so we can know them no matter what happens to us as we try to follow you, even when we have to be hurt, even when we have to give up, and even when we have to die.

Help us, O Lord, never to give in to an attitude that presumes upon those mercies as if we are entitled to them or that pursues them outside the parameters of what constitutes a life lived in the following of Jesus Christ, who came not to save his life but to give it away.

Amen.

DAY 39: GOD'S WAY

Then the devil brought him to a very high mountain and showed him all the kingdoms of the world and their glory. He said, "I'll give you all these if you bow down and worship me." Jesus responded, 'Go away, Satan, because it's written, You will worship the Lord your God and serve only him.' The devil left him, and angels came and took care of him. (Matthew 4:8-11 CEB)

Doing things Satan's way may seem to have certain advantages, but they are all temporary and ultimately lead nowhere. Besides, to give our allegiance to Satan requires us to live in his ways. Sure, we may gain a lot of wealth, power, and prestige, but we'll be obligated to put ourselves above others and acquisitions above relationships. We'll hurt a lot of people on our way to the top, and we'll ultimately destroy ourselves. On the other hand, to give our allegiance to God means to do things in God's way, which makes God's spiritual and moral resources available to us. We'll be obligated to put others above self and relationships above acquisitions. But we'll love and help a lot of people along the way.

O God, we want to worship and serve only you. Help us turn away from the devil's ways of putting possessions, power, and prestige above everything and everyone else. Help us keep our eyes, hearts, and minds so focused on you that our only desire is to live as you would have us live and do what you would have us do. Inspire us with Jesus' total commitment to you. Help us never forget that while living in Jesus' way is challenging and costly, it is the only way to real life. It is the only way to truly worship and serve you. Help us be aware of and take in the spiritual nourishment you send us. May it strengthen us to live out your way for us. Amen.

DAY 40: TIMING

Now when Jesus heard that John was arrested, he went to Galilee. (Matthew 4:12, CEB)

Jesus responded to the changing circumstances around him. He made decisions about what to do based on what was happening in his environment. He was sensitive to what was happening in the world around him, and he responded in light of that sensitivity.

Help us, O Lord, to pay attention. Help us to be sensitive to what's happening around us and to the possible implications of those happenings for the living of our lives and for our service to you and to others.

Then help us make our decisions and carry out our actions based on what seems best, not just for ourselves but for our role and responsibility in your kingdom.

Perhaps Jesus withdrew at the time of John's arrest because he perceived a danger to himself. There would come a time when he would not withdraw but would instead place himself directly in the path of danger.

Give us, O Lord, a similar sense of your timing as we make our decisions.

Amen.

DAY 41: LIGHT IN THE DARKNESS

He left Nazareth and settled in Capernaum, which lies alongside the sea in the area of Zebulun and Naphtali. This fulfilled what Isaiah the prophet said: Land of Zebulun and land of Naphtali, alongside the sea, across the Jordan, Galilee of the Gentiles, the people who lived in the dark have seen a great light, and a light has come upon those who lived in the region and in shadow of death. (Matthew 4:13-16, CEB)

Jesus, by his very presence in the world, brought light into the darkness, light that dispelled the shadow of death.

He still does.

God, this world still struggles with darkness. We who live in it still struggle with the shadow of death. Open our lives up to the light of Jesus that will, by your grace, dispel the darkness of anxiety, fear, and dread.

Grant that we who have experienced and received that light will reflect it just enough so that others might catch a glimpse of it through us and be able to turn toward it themselves.

Amen.

DAY 42: GOD'S REIGN

From that time Jesus began to announce, "Change your hearts and lives! Here comes the kingdom of heaven!" (Matthew 4:17, CEB)

In Jesus, the kingdom of heaven, the reign of God, broke into this world in a way that was at the same time majestic and intimate, revealed and hidden, and complex and simple.

The kingdom is still here, and it is still all those things.

It makes a difference now, as it made a difference then, that those who are able and willing receive the grace through faith that opens their lives up to the fact of God and to the attendant facts of God's love, God's mercy, God's will, and God's way.

O God, make us able and willing.

O God, turn us evermore to you and away from everything that is not you.

Amen.

DAY 43: BEING SEEN

As Jesus walked alongside the Galilee Sea, he saw two brothers, Simon, who is called Peter, and Andrew, throwing fishing nets into the sea, because they were fishermen. (Matthew 4:18, CEB)

He sees us where we are, doing whatever we are doing for whatever reasons we are doing it.

He sees us as we are, regardless of the choices or the circumstances that have made us who we are.

In the course of being who he is, he sees us in the course of being who we are.

We value being seen, being noticed, being taken into account by those around us—how much more so by the Lord of the universe and the Savior of the world.

Thank you, Jesus, for seeing us.
Amen.

DAY 44: DEVELOPMENT

"Come, follow me," he said, "and I'll show you how to fish for people." (Matthew 4:19, CEB)

The Lord Jesus sees us as we are, takes us as we are, and uses us as we are. And, if we follow him and are open to him, he develops us into the best version of ourselves that we can be, a version of ourselves that will touch people with the grace of God and with the love of Christ that will flow freely into us, through us, and from us.

Jesus, give us the desire and the will to follow you wherever you lead and into whatever developments in our character and in our approach to life that need to happen for us to be the best conduits of grace and love to those around us that we can be.
Amen.

DAY 45: LEAVE

Right away, they left their nets and followed him. (Matthew 4:20, CEB)

Lord, give us the courage to leave what we need to leave to follow you.

There may be sinful things we need to leave to follow you. But there may also be good things we need to leave to follow you; there may be things that have done right by us and through which we have done right by others that nonetheless now stand in the way of our being who we need to be and doing what we need to do.

There may be tried and true ways of living that just won't work anymore—not, at least, if we want to follow you.

So help us, Lord, to leave behind what we need to leave behind to follow you.

And help us to do so immediately, since the one moment we know we have is this one.

Amen.

DAY 46: OTHERS

Continuing on, he saw another set of brothers, James the son of Zebedee and his brother John. They were in a boat with Zebedee their father repairing their nets. Jesus called them . . . . (Matthew 4:21, CEB)

There are always others.

Jesus always sees others and he always calls others. He had already called Peter and Andrew. But Peter and Andrew would just have to understand that they were not enough. Jesus also needed James and John—and dozens and hundreds and thousands and millions of others that he has seen and still sees and has called and still calls.

Lord, if we have felt your gaze and heard your call, thank you. But protect us from the pride that tells us that we are more important than we are or that we need less partnership with others than we do.

Lord, if we feel your gaze and hear your call, thank you. Lead us to follow you, and in following you to walk and work gladly beside the others whom you have seen and called.

After all, you and we need all the sisters and brothers we can get.

Amen.

DAY 47: LEAVING

. . . immediately they left the boat and their father and followed him. (Matthew 4:22, CEB)

It's not hard to imagine Zebedee standing there, net in hand, shouting after his sons and partners in the family business, "Hey—where do you think you're going?"

It's also not hard to imagine him standing there, net in hand, mouth open, not knowing what to say.

It's also not hard to imagine him standing there, net in hand, wishing he could go, too.

James and John did leave their father, though, didn't they?

O God, this is a hard prayer to pray.

Help us have the faith and the courage to leave our father, mother, sister, brother, or anyone else we need to leave behind in order to do what we need to for you.

We can never leave them completely behind; we always carry them with us. But if going with you means going without them, help us do so.

Maybe the harder thing, Lord, is to have to leave them even if we stay where they are—to find it necessary to be different than they are and to live differently than they do right there in their town and right there under their noses. Maybe that takes even greater faith and courage.

But Lord, maybe our leaving them, whether we physically stay or go, can be the catalyst that leads them to follow you, too.

It would be great, Lord, if we could all go together.

Amen.

DAY 48: THROUGHOUT

Jesus traveled throughout Galilee, teaching in their synagogues. He announced the good news of the kingdom and healed every disease and sickness among the people. (Matthew 4:23, CEB)

Jesus went throughout Galilee. Everywhere he went he taught, he preached, and he healed.

It's a good model for how the body of Christ, the church, should live out its life and carry out its ministry today. We are to live our lives in the area where we are—and, given how small the world is getting with our modes of travel and means of communication, our "area" is less and less limited—and everywhere we go we are to share the good news of Jesus Christ, the good news that, with our words and actions, offers and delivers acceptance, wholeness, and wellness to lost, sick, and broken people.

O God, help us pay attention to where we are and to the people who are all around us. Help us also be willing to go beyond the perceived borders of "our" area and to reach out in love to the people we find as we go.

As we go, help us speak, act, and touch in ways that communicate your love, grace, and healing to everyone we meet.

Amen.

DAY 49: FAME

News about him spread throughout Syria. People brought to him all those who had various kinds of diseases, those in pain, those possessed by demons, those with epilepsy, and those who were paralyzed, and he healed them. Large crowds followed him from Galilee, the Decapolis, Jerusalem, Judea, and from the areas beyond the Jordan River. (Matthew 4:24-25, CEB)

Fame and crowds attached themselves to Jesus because of his acts of healing. Those acts demonstrated the presence of God and were driven by the power of God's grace, love, and mercy.

Later, though, Jesus would demonstrate God's presence, power, grace, love, and mercy in ways that would turn his fans who considered him famous into foes who considered him infamous.

God, give us grace and wisdom not to put too much stock in the ways that our ministry and service do or don't impress people.

Give us grace and wisdom not to evaluate the effectiveness or validity of our ministry and service by the ways in which people do or don't respond to us.

Give us grace and wisdom—and courage—to understand that sometimes people will respond well when our ministry and service are not Christ-like, and that sometimes they will respond badly when our ministry and service are Christ-like.

And if fame does come our way, don't let us quite believe it.

Amen.

DAY 50: CROWDS

When Jesus saw the crowds, he went up the mountain .... (Matthew 5:1a, NRSV)

Great crowds were following Jesus.

Great crowds have great needs. Jesus had been healing people, and no doubt he could have spent every minute of every day dealing with disease and with other devastating factors in the people's lives.

So Jesus looked at the great crowd that was following him, the great crowd with its endless needs—and he turned around and walked up a mountain. He changed his location, his position, and his perspective. By so doing he changed the location, the position, and the perspective of the crowds.

Lord, as the body of Christ in the world today, we who are the church have a responsibility toward the crowds. We have a responsibility to deal with their hurts and needs—to deal with their lives—with your grace, love, and Spirit.

Give us discernment and wisdom to know when, faced with such great need as we perpetually are, it is time to make a shift in our location, in our position, and in our perspective—for their sake and for ours.

For in making the shifts that we must make, we may lead them to make the ones that they must make—and we might all then see you more clearly.

Amen.

DAY 51: COMING TO JESUS

And after he sat down, his disciples came to him. (Matthew 5:1b, NRSV)

It seems so simple and so basic, but it is so important: "his disciples came to him."

What if they hadn't? Then they would have missed the confounding and compelling words that Jesus was about to speak. They would have missed an experience of fellowship with him and of learning from him that could and no doubt did make a tremendous difference for them.

God, it seems odd to ask you to inspire us to come to Jesus. After all, if we are his disciples, shouldn't we naturally want to come to him? Apparently, based on what we have shown so far in our lives, we do need such inspiration. So please give it to us.

God, help us develop the discipline of continually coming to Jesus to fellowship with him, to learn from him, and to submit to him. Help us come to Jesus every moment of every day, but help us also seek and set aside particular times of every day, of every week, and of every year in which we make a determined effort to come to him.

God, in your great grace you caused Jesus to come to us. In your great grace you allow us to come to him. Cause us to praise you for your grace by taking advantage of the privileges and responsibilities that you in your grace have given us.

Amen.

DAY 52: LISTEN

Then he began to speak, and taught them, saying . . . .
(Matthew 5:2, NRSV)

The words that follow this line constitute what we call the Sermon on the Mount, which is perhaps the most inspiring and challenging collection of teachings ever gathered in one place.

These amazing words, though, are only a portion of the words of Jesus collected in the Gospels, and we can safely assume that the words of Jesus found in the Gospels are only a fraction of the teachings given by Jesus during his life on earth. We trust that our Bibles preserve the words of Jesus that we need to hear, to know, and to do.

Cause us, O God, to take the words of Jesus with more seriousness than we do any other words, since those words come from the One who was the Word that was with God and that was God and that became flesh and dwelt among us, full of grace and truth (John 1).

Cause us, O God, to be able to hear the teachings of Jesus that still come to us through the presence of your Holy Spirit with us, teachings that are perhaps more likely to come to us in the sense of guidance in the ways we should feel, think, talk, and act than in any other form.

Cause us, O God, to be formed and shaped by the spoken and written words of Jesus and by the influence of the living Word who is Jesus into the best version of ourselves that we can be.

But before any of that, O God, cause us to listen to Jesus.

Amen.

DAY 53: POOR IN SPIRIT

"Blessed are the poor in spirit, for theirs is the kingdom of heaven." (Matthew 5:3, NRSV)

Those who are poor in spirit realize that they are lacking and know that they are needy. They therefore are open to receive what they need from

God to find fulfillment. Those who aren't poor in spirit don't admit their lack, don't face their need, and therefore are closed to receiving what can fulfill them.

Those who are poor in spirit are humble without being humiliated, poverty-stricken without being pitiable, and self-aware without being self-consumed. Those who are not poor in spirit are rich in pride, endowed with foolishness, and full of self.

O Lord, make our true poverty so clear to us that we can't help but see it. Reveal our true need to us so we can't help but admit it. Replace our false pride with true humility so we can't help but live out of it.

Then, use our awareness of our true spiritual state as a conduit through which your grace, which constitutes the essence of your kingdom, can flow into our lives and then flow back out of us to others who also realize their spiritual lack and are as desperate as we are to be filled with what matters.

Amen.

DAY 54: MOURNFUL

"Blessed are those who mourn, for they will be comforted." (Matthew 5:4, NRSV)

We mourn when we lose someone or something. We mourn because we sense the absence of someone or something that used to be there or that should be there.

Those who mourn are blessed because those who mourn face their losses and their empty places honestly and openly, rather than living with false bravado and feigned invulnerability.

Those who mourn are blessed because those who mourn accept the comfort they need, rather than pretending that they don't need it and thus depriving themselves of it.

Those who mourn are blessed because they practice accepting the grace they need in the here and now that will make them especially ready to receive the grace that will come to them in the there and then.

Those who mourn are blessed because they embrace, with great faith and hope, the fact that they are not all that they should, could, or will be, along with the fact that God will work in their lives to give them the comfort of ever-increasing wholeness and—one blessed day—absolute and complete wholeness.

O God, we mourn what we are not.
O God, we accept what we are.
O God, we live toward what we will be.
Amen.

DAY 55: MEEK

"Blessed are the meek, for they will inherit the earth."
(Matthew 5:5, NRSV)

To be meek is not to be mild. The Lord Jesus was meek, but we would hardly regard him as mild.

Indeed, no greater strength can be displayed than that which is displayed through meekness. No one ever displayed greater meekness and thus greater strength than Jesus did.

To be meek is to be willing and able to accept and absorb the harm or wrong that someone inflicts on you, and thereby perhaps to redeem it, to turn it into something positive for the community or the world—and maybe even for the one or ones inflicting the harm.

Perhaps there is no greater form of meekness than to be willing and able to take and absorb the harm or wrong that someone inflicts not on you but rather on another—or on many others—and thus to redeem it.

It is hard to imagine a characteristic that is more Christlike than meekness.

So, God, give us the vision to see beyond the present hurt.

Give us the faith to see how you might work in it, through it, and beyond it to bring about something better.

Give us the courage to be meek and the meekness to be courageous.
Amen.

DAY 56: RIGHTEOUSNESS

"Blessed are those who hunger and thirst for righteousness, for they will be filled." (Matthew 5:6, NRSV)

We hunger for food and we thirst for water because we must have food and water to live.

We are blessed if we hunger and thirst for righteousness, for a sound and whole relationship with God that develops into a similar relationship with ourselves and with each other. Like we hunger and thirst for food and water, we realize that we just can't live without relationship with God.

We cannot be blessed, then, if we can live our lives without a craving for such relationships that leads us to do everything we can to experience them.

Lord, as paradoxical as it may sound, fill us with a hunger and a thirst for righteousness.

Lord, deliver us from the frustration that will come to us if we think we can satisfy that hunger and thirst for ourselves. Help us instead to depend on you to satisfy them.

And Lord, cause us, as we experience some satisfying of our hunger and thirst for righteousness, to share what we have gained with others who are similarly hungry and thirsty.

Amen.

DAY 57: MERCIFUL

"Blessed are the merciful, for they will receive mercy." (Matthew 5:7, NRSV)

Mercy leads to mercy, which leads to mercy, which leads to mercy, and so on.

O God, we celebrate and praise you for the mercy that you have lavished upon us. For you, in your holiness, to extend such grace to us that we are accepted and forgiven by you is incredible, especially when we know that we did nothing—indeed, that we can do nothing—to deserve it.

Remind us, we ask, even in our embarrassment at having to ask, to rejoice in your mercy.

O God, we acknowledge that the reception of such mercy does, or at least should, motivate and move us to extend mercy to those who have wronged or hurt us. After all, any affront committed against us by a peer can hardly compare to those committed by us against you.

Empower us, we ask, even as we repent of our failures to do so, to lavish mercy on others as it has been lavished on us.

O God, we acknowledge that, as we receive your mercy and as we extend your mercy to others, we become more and more able to receive mercy both from you and from other people.

Open us, we ask, even as we mourn the ways and places that we are closed, better to have your mercy flow into us and then out of us to others.

After all, mercy leads to mercy, which leads to mercy, which leads to mercy, and so on.

Amen.

DAY 58: PURE IN HEART

"Blessed are the pure in heart, for they will see God."
(Matthew 5:8, NRSV)

In one of the more interesting paradoxes in life, you, O God, are everywhere, but we have to know where to look to see you.

And the key to knowing where to look is to look from the right vantage point.

Give us, O God, pure hearts—hearts, wills, and lives that want one thing and one thing only: to know you—because it is from the vantage point of that one desire that we can see you.

We look forward to the day when we will have absolute purity of heart and we will see you face to face.

But cause us to grow in singleness of heart here and now, day by day, moment by moment, blessing by blessing, and crisis by crisis, so that we might see you more and more clearly with each passing second.

Thank you that each time we see you a little more clearly, our hearts become a little purer.

Amen.

DAY 59: PEACEMAKERS

"Blessed are the peacemakers, for they will be called children of God." (Matthew 5:9, NRSV)

If we wait until we have complete peace in our own lives—meaning absolute wholeness in our relationship with God, with ourselves, and with others—to work for peace in our families, in our churches, in our communities, in our nation, and in our world, then we won't work for peace until we get to heaven, and the effort would then be, to say the least, superfluous.

So God, thank you for the peace that you have brought about in our lives, in process though it may be.

Help us, God, to know that we do have to work for peace prayerfully and faithfully, to work for increased wholeness and soundness in the hearts, lives, and relationships of everybody we can, and especially of the person or people in whose presence we happen to be at the moment.

To be peacemakers is to bear a strong family resemblance to our brother Jesus who was and is, after all, the Prince of Peace.

Help us to look, through our efforts at bringing about peace, more and more like your children every day.

Amen.

DAY 60: PERSECUTED

*"Blessed are those who are persecuted for righteousness'
sake, for theirs is the kingdom of heaven."* (Matthew
5:10, NRSV)

There are people all over the world who are being persecuted—truly
persecuted—for righteousness' sake, for the sake of their faithful witness
to their relationship with God and to the ways of God's kingdom. Some
are economically marginalized, some are attacked, some are imprisoned,
and some are executed.

O God, thank you for the blessings of the persecuted, given both
because of the joy they find in their faithful testimony to you in the
present and because of the utter joy they will find when they are in your
presence in the future. Keep them safe and protect them from harm. No
matter what comes to them, give them the strength to be faithful.

O God, give those of us who live in places where freedom of religious
expression is the norm the perspective and the class to acknowledge that
the little slights and even the large criticisms we receive for our faith do
not rise to a level where they can be classified as persecution.

At the same time, so fill us with your grace, love, peace, joy, and
mercy that it will be obvious to all those around us, if such persecution
ever comes here, that it should come to us.

Amen.

DAY 61: REVILED

*"Blessed are you when people revile you and persecute
you and utter all kinds of evil against you falsely on my
account. Rejoice and be glad, for your reward is great in
heaven, for in the same way they persecuted the prophets
who were before you."* (Matthew 5:11-12, NRSV)

O God, please give us grace and wisdom to remember a few important things.

First, help us remember that when people talk behind our backs or criticize us to our faces because we are Christians, it usually does not, at least in American or Western culture, rise to the level of our being reviled or persecuted.

Second, help us remember that sometimes when we are criticized, the criticism is justified, even if we are being criticized for allegedly Christian attitudes or behaviors. It is possible, after all, to be "religious" in the worst sense of the word. Jesus said we are blessed when people revile us and persecute us and utter all kinds of evil against us falsely, not truthfully.

Third, help us remember that Jesus said we are blessed when people revile us and persecute us and utter all kinds of evil against us falsely on his account. In other words, we are blessed when we are persecuted or lied about because we think, talk, and act in ways that are like the ways Jesus thought, talked, and acted. Help us to take seriously this question: what are the chances that we would be reviled or persecuted because our thoughts, words, and actions have been too gracious, too forgiving, too merciful, too truthful, and too loving?

Fourth, help us remember that a martyr complex is unbecoming, even as you help us remember that martyrdom comes to people who don't seek it but who, when it comes, accept it.

Finally, help us be as in tune with you as your prophets were so that, whether we suffer here or rejoice there, we will always know the joy of your presence.

Amen.

DAY 62: SALT OF THE EARTH

"You are the salt of the earth; but if salt has lost its taste, how can its saltiness be restored? It is no longer good for anything, but is thrown out and trampled under foot."
(Matthew 5:13, NRSV)

Salt makes things taste salty; if it doesn't make things taste salty, it isn't salt. When you stop and think about it, non-salty salt is useless because it isn't what it is.

God, help us always to be what we are, namely, faithful disciples of Jesus whose motives, words, and actions permeate our homes, our churches, our neighborhoods, our communities, our towns, our cities, our states, our nation, and our world with the grace, love, and peace of our Lord.
Amen.

DAY 63: LIGHT OF THE WORLD

"You are the light of the world. A city built on a hill cannot be hid. No one after lighting a lamp puts it under the bushel basket, but on the lampstand, and it gives light to all in the house. In the same way, let your light shine before others, so that they may see your good works and give glory to your Father in heaven." (Matthew 5:14-16, NRSV)

Lord, form us into reflectors of light. May the light that people see in us come from you so that it will be good and true light that will lead people in the way you would have them go.

Lord, form us into deflectors of light. May the light that people see in us, which comes from you anyway, be deflected to shine clearly on you so that they might come to know your light in their own lives.

Lord, form us into people who neither hide nor hoard the light.
Amen.

DAY 64: FULFILL

"Do not think that I have come to abolish the law or the prophets; I have come not to abolish but to fulfill. For truly I tell you, until heaven and earth pass away, not a letter, not one stroke of a letter, will pass from the law until all is accomplished." (Matthew 5:17-18, NRSV)

All of us, whether we recognize or acknowledge it, have a worldview, a way of looking at and interpreting reality that conditions our responses and reactions to people, to events, and to our thoughts and feelings.

Lord, does our worldview coalesce with our identity as people who follow Jesus Christ? He is, after all, the One in whom all things are fulfilled and in whom all things will be accomplished. He is, after all, the One who is the center of all things and through whom all things can best be perceived, understood, and approached.

Forgive us, Lord, when we let a competing worldview have more influence in our lives than the worldview we should have as disciples of Jesus Christ.

Help us, Lord, to see Jesus as the interpretive key that, in time and through faith, has, does, and will unlock everything.

Amen.

DAY 65: DOING AND TEACHING

"Therefore, whoever breaks one of the least of these commandments, and teaches others to do the same, will be called least in the kingdom of heaven; but whoever does them and teaches them will be called great in the kingdom of heaven." (Matthew 5:19, NRSV)

Perhaps no line can be drawn between doing and teaching; maybe the best way—maybe even the only way—we teach somebody something is by doing it ourselves. This much is clear: the right words don't matter much if they aren't backed up by the right actions.

O God, help us to be people who teach by our actions; help us be people who by the way we live our lives provide a sound example to those around us, offering an accurate reflection of who you are.

O God, help us use our lives to teach the ways of Jesus Christ our Lord, in whose actions, words, death, and resurrection we see the fulfillment of the way you mean things to be.

Amen.

DAY 66: RIGHTEOUSNESS, PLUS

"For I tell you, unless your righteousness exceeds that of the scribes and Pharisees, you will never enter the kingdom of heaven." (Matthew 5:20, NRSV)

In their day, there were probably no people around who were more "righteous" than the scribes and Pharisees, at least when it came to knowing what the Bible said and making every effort to follow its teaching.

Jesus seems to be saying, then, that being his disciples and gaining entry into the kingdom of heaven require that we do more than know what the Bible says.

Somehow, O God, we must let you help us get to the heart, to the spirit, to the essence of it all. Somehow, O God, we must grow to live out a relationship with you that forms not only our actions but also our motives, our attitudes, and our relationships.

Work in us, O God, so that we become every day more of who you mean for us to be in order to do more of what you mean for us to do, not only because the Bible says so but also because our relationship with you causes that way of life to be more and more natural to us.

Amen.

DAY 67: ANGRY

"You have heard that it was said to those of ancient times, 'You shall not murder'; and 'whoever murders shall be liable to judgment.' But I say to you that if you are angry with a brother or sister, you will be liable to judgment; and if you insult a brother or sister, you will be liable to the council; and if you say, 'You fool,' you will be liable to the hell of fire." (Matthew 5:21-22, NRSV)

The chances that we will murder somebody are thankfully slim. The chances that we will get angry enough at someone to want them dead or hurt or at least knocked down a few notches are regretfully great.

So, Lord, work in our hearts to take away the negative and dangerous attitudes we sometimes harbor toward others.

But that's not enough.

Lord, work in our hearts to cause us to grow in respect, in care, in compassion, in mercy, and in love for other people—and especially for those who hurt us or who do things that make us angry.

We pray these things most earnestly, Lord, because clearly we can't make such outlandish progress on our own.

Amen.

DAY 68: RECONCILIATION

"So when you are offering your gift at the altar, if you remember that your brother or sister has something against you, leave your gift there before the altar and

go; first be reconciled to your brother or sister, and then come and offer your gift." (Matthew 5:23, NRSV)

In God's way of looking at things, our relationship with the Other and our relationship with others are closely connected.

God, forgive our efforts to compartmentalize our relationships, for our tendency to kid ourselves into thinking that somehow things can be right with you, whom we have never seen, when they are wrong with the sibling we see every day.

God, forgive our efforts to compartmentalize our worship, our tendency to kid ourselves into thinking that somehow we can lay our lives before you in the sanctuary when we refuse to lay our lives before each other in our daily lives.

God, as we revel in the truth that Jesus Christ through his death and resurrection reconciled us to you, cause us to grow in the related truth that we are to be reconciled to each other. Give us the grace both to seek reconciliation with another and to accept reconciliation that another seeks from us.

Amen.

DAY 69: COMING TO TERMS

"Come to terms quickly with your accuser while you are on the way to court with him, or your accuser may hand you over to the judge, and the judge to the guard, and you will be thrown into prison. Truly I tell you, you will never get out until you have paid the last penny." (Matthew 5:25-26, NRSV)

We who are citizens of the kingdom of heaven still have to live in the real world, and in that real world, relationships can become frazzled, damaged, and even broken.

Sometimes we don't deserve the anger someone feels toward us or the accusations someone brings against us.

But sometimes we do.

O Lord, when we do deserve them, give us the strength of character to acknowledge our fault and to embrace our responsibility. Then, inspire us to take steps to make things right with the one or ones whom we have wronged.

Let us be motivated by a desire to be faithful to who you are, to who we are in you, and to who our fellow people are to us because of you.

Amen.

DAY 70: LUST

"You have heard that it was said, 'You shall not commit adultery.' But I say to you that everyone who looks at a woman with lust has already committed adultery with her in his heart." (Matthew 5:27-28, NRSV)

To pray that we will not look on another person with lust in our hearts is to pray for several things at once.

So let us pray.

God, help us see people as people and not as objects to be used for our own gratification.

God, help us seek relationships with people that are meaningful and enduring rather than shallow and selfish.

God, help us develop hearts that want to care about other people and to cultivate healthy relationships with them.

God, help us be empowered by your love and grace to give our lives to developing the real relationships that we have rather than to expend our mental and emotional energy in distracting fantasies.

God, help us celebrate the good gift of our sexuality through its healthy expression in a relationship that is based in a lifelong commitment to you and to each other.

God, help us be sound and mature adults in the ways we think about and behave toward other people and in the ways we think about and behave toward ourselves.

Amen.

DAY 71: EYES AND HANDS

"If your right eye causes you to sin, tear it out and throw it away; it is better for you to lose one of your members than for your whole body to be thrown into hell. And if your right hand causes you to sin, cut it off and throw it away; it is better for you to lose one of your members than for your whole body to go into hell." (Matthew 5:29-30, NRSV)

I think it was Gandhi who first pointed out that the logical end of "an eye for an eye and a tooth for a tooth" is a blind and toothless society.

In the same way, the logical end of the literal application of Jesus' words here is a Christian population with no eyes and no hands.

It is possible that Jesus was making his point through the use of absurdity and indirection. He could have meant something like, "Of course your eye and your hand are going to cause you to sin, but what are you going to do about it—rip out your eye and cut off your hand? Better, then, to concentrate on the state of your heart, from which your sinful attitudes sprout and from which your sinful actions emerge."

It is also possible that Jesus was making his point through the use of hyperbole. He could have meant something like, "Lustful looks lead to adulterous actions, and so if you find yourself falling prey to such sins, it's serious business and you should do anything you can to avoid them. It's so serious that I can describe the lengths to which you should go to avoid them in terms like ripping your eye out and cutting your hand off. But for goodness' sake, don't take me literally."

Regardless of Jesus' rhetorical method here, his point is clear: we should take very, very, very seriously our responsibility to let God, in

God's grace and love, develop hearts in us that want to view people in the right way and to treat people in the right way.

So, God, work that great work in us. Help us every day to treat the people we encounter with a little more love, a little more grace, and a little more respect.
Amen.

DAY 72: MARRIAGE

"It was also said, 'Whoever divorces his wife, let him give her a certificate of divorce.' But I say to you that anyone who divorces his wife, except on the ground of unchastity, causes her to commit adultery; and whoever marries a divorced woman commits adultery."
(Matthew 5:31-32, NRSV)

As we grow in our awareness of what it means to be followers of Jesus Christ, we will come more and more to live lives that are characterized by the constant desire to put the needs of others ahead of our own needs and by a deep concern over the ways that our motives, attitudes, and actions affect other people.

So Jesus, speaking in a time when men could secure a divorce with ease while women could not, and in a time when the accepted practices of marriage and divorce created an atmosphere in which men were tempted to treat women as property and women were tempted to accept such treatment as normal, focused on the responsibility of the men who had the upper hand toward the women who were easily victimized.

These days, at least in many cultures, his words would need to be applied to both partners in a marriage relationship.

O God, help us have marriages that are marked by a commitment to one another that is based on our commitment to you.

O God, help us treat each other in our marriages with love, respect, and concern.

O God, help us in our marriages to put the needs of the other ahead of ours.

O God, help us in our marriages not only to do no harm to one another but also to do great good for one another.

Amen.

DAY 73: SWEARING

"Again, you have heard that it was said to those of ancient times, 'You shall not swear falsely, but carry out the vows you have made to the Lord.' But I say to you, Do not swear at all, either by heaven, for it is the throne of God, or by the earth, for it is his footstool, or by Jerusalem, for it is the city of the great King. And do not swear by your head, for you cannot make one hair white or black." (Matthew 5:33-36, NRSV)

At least part of Jesus' meaning seems to be that it is pointless to swear by anything that doesn't belong to us, that we don't control, and the destiny of which isn't in our hands—and that eliminates our swearing by anything.

Lord, keep us constantly mindful of the fact that everything belongs to you, that we are recipients of your great blessings, and that we are stewards and caretakers of your great creation.

Guard us from arrogance that would cause us to use what does not belong to us as collateral to support our standing and our statements.

Guard us as well from a tendency to inflate falsely the value and meaning of our words by appealing to an authority outside ourselves.

Cause us to grow in our awareness of who we are and who we aren't so our words will come from the center of our being, which will be authority enough.

Amen.

DAY 74: OUR WORD

"Let your word be 'Yes, Yes,' or 'No, No'; anything more than this comes from the evil one." (Matthew 5:37, NRSV)

I had just concluded a statement with the words, "Really, I mean it." A friend asked me, "So, if you don't say you mean what you said, does that mean you didn't mean it?"

I had never thought before about how important it is that my word stand on its own without need of other words to prop it up. It boils down to the simple truth that people need to be able to believe what I say because I say it and because my character, which is supposed to be conforming more and more to the image of Christ, reveals itself in my integrity.

God, help us grow in our character to the point that our words are honest and sound because wholeness and integrity characterize our lives.

May the strength of our character be so obvious to everyone around us that they can assume the honesty of our words. May the words that come out of our mouths match up so well with the actions that come out of our lives that everyone can count on our integrity.

Amen.

DAY 75: RESISTANCE

"You have heard that it was said, 'An eye for an eye and a tooth for a tooth.' But I say to you, Do not resist an evil-doer. But if anyone strikes you on the right cheek, turn the other also; and if anyone wants to sue you and take your coat, give your cloak as well. And if anyone forces you to go one mile, go also the second mile." (Matthew 5:38-41, NRSV)

Forgive our desire to explain away these hard words, O Lord.

Give us grace to accept them and strength to live them.

At the heart of these challenging words of Jesus seems to be that we who follow him are called to move beyond a focus on what others would take from us to a more radical focus on what we can give to others. Our desire to give, to offer, to share, and to sacrifice should extend even to those who would and do take from us and make demands of us.

Perhaps we are supposed to overcome evil with good, to overcome taking with giving, to overcome aggression with nonviolent resistance, and to overcome demands with offers.

It is likely that all of us praying this prayer have a long way to go, O Lord, so help us make a little progress today. After all, a little bit of this kind of grace, especially as it shows itself in our attitudes and actions toward our enemies, will go a long, long way in this old world.

Amen.

DAY 76: GIVING

"Give to everyone who begs from you, and do not refuse anyone who wants to borrow from you." (Matthew 5:42, NRSV)

Our default setting is to keep and to refuse rather than to give and to loan.

Forgive us, O Lord, for our hard hearts, for our hard heads, and for our hard ways.

Forgive us for living in the oxymoronic state of being "selfish Christians."

Fill us with the grace, love, and sacrificial spirit of Jesus Christ our Lord, who not only spoke these difficult words but also lived—in the most extreme way—the kind of difficult life that gives meaning, power, and authority to his words.

Fill us with a Christlike generosity that, as big a thing as it may seem to us, is but the smallest evidence of a Christlike life.

Amen.

DAY 77: LOVING

"You have heard that it was said, 'You shall love your neighbor and hate your enemies.' But I say to you, Love your enemies and pray for those who persecute you, so that you may be children of your Father in heaven; for he makes his sun rise on the evil and on the good, and sends rain on the righteous and on the unrighteous."
(Matthew 5:43-45, NRSV)

What an honor it would be to look like our heavenly Father looks, to think and to act like our heavenly Father thinks and acts, and to treat people like our heavenly Father treats people.

According to Jesus, one way we do so is by loving and praying for everybody, including our enemies, because our heavenly Father sends blessings on everybody, including those who don't want to relate to God or who stand in opposition to God.

O God, it will take a lot of intervention on your part—quite an infusion of grace, love, and mercy—for us to develop such a family resemblance. Please break our hearts open, if that's what it takes, so that we can receive your gifts that will in turn compel us to share them—yes, even with, and even especially with, our enemies.

Amen.

DAY 78: MORE

"For if you love those who love you, what reward do you have? Do not even the tax collectors do the same? And if you greet only your brothers and sisters, what more are you doing than others? Do not even the Gentiles do the same?" (Matthew 5:46-47, NRSV)

On one hand, and in other places, Jesus warns us against comparing ourselves favorably to others. He warns us against an attitude that leads to prayers like, "God, I thank you that I am not like other people," because such an attitude indicates that we are far, far from the humility that opens us up and keeps us opened to God's grace.

On the other hand, and in this place, Jesus instructs us to compare ourselves to others with the aim of encouraging us to be better than and to do better than other people are and do.

O God, give us discernment to know the difference between, on the one hand, a lack of humility that causes us to think we're better than other people and, on the other hand, an acceptance of your grace that causes us to embrace the challenge to be and do more than we would able to be and do apart from your grace.

O God, give us insight to know and live in the truth that the one thing at which we are called to be and do better than other people is love. We are to love other people, even our enemies, and we are to be hospitable to other people, even our enemies, in ways that would be impossible apart from the presence of your love and grace in us.

Perhaps one of the keys to the whole thing is that this "superior" stance toward life and style of life will help not only us but also everyone with whom we come into contact. In a way, then, it's still more about others than it is about us.

O God, help us love like we are capable of loving because your love is present in our lives.

Amen.

DAY 79: PERFECT

"Be perfect, therefore, as your heavenly Father is perfect."
(Matthew 5:48, NRSV)

This command of Jesus is terribly intimidating even when we realize that "perfect" means "whole" or "complete" or "mature," and even when we realize that, given the context within which this saying occurs, our perfection is to be perfection in showing love to all, even to our enemies.

After all, we all know how divided, incomplete, and immature we are even when we are at our best. We furthermore know how far we have to go in loving others like God loves them.

So Lord, please help us.

Help us know that we can grow every day toward greater maturity in the love we show to the people around us, even to those who don't love us.

Help us know that, if we will submit ourselves to the working of your grace, love, and Spirit and to the intentional and determined following of Jesus Christ, we can make a little progress every day so that, by the time we're done, we may have just about made it.

Amen.

DAY 80: SEEN

"Beware of practicing your piety before others in order to be seen by them; for then you have no reward from your Father in heaven." (Matthew 6:1, NRSV)

In this place Jesus says, "Beware of practicing your piety before others in order to be seen by them." But in another place Jesus said, "Let your light shine before others, so that they may see your good works and give glory to your Father in heaven" (Matthew 5:16).

On one hand, then, we are not to let others see our good works.

On the other hand, though, we are to let others see our good works.

The difference between letting others see our good works in a good way and letting others see our good works in a bad way apparently comes down to our motivation. Do we want people to see what we do so they'll notice what good people we are? Or do we want people to see what we do so they'll notice what a great God we serve?

It is hard for us to stay on the right side of that line.

O God, help us know where the line is between witness and display and between righteousness and self-righteousness.

Give us grace to live on the side of witness and righteousness.
Amen.

DAY 81: IN SECRET

*"So whenever you give alms, do not sound a trumpet
before you, as the hypocrites do in the synagogues and in
the streets, so that they may be praised by others. Truly I
tell you, they have received their reward. But when you
give alms, do not let your left hand know what your right
hand is doing, so that your alms may be done in secret;
and your Father who sees in secret will reward you."*
(Matthew 6:2-4, NRSV)

Jesus doesn't say how God will reward us for the giving we do in secret.

He does make it clear, however, that we should not give in ways that
would cause others to give us credit or that would even allow us to give
ourselves credit.

It stands to reason that whatever rewards we get from God—which
may well have to do with the peace that comes from not feeling like we
have to prove our worth to others or to ourselves or even to God by any
means, including a public display of "generosity"—will be greater than
any pat on the back we could get from other people or from ourselves.

O God, give us hearts that want to share what we have for the sake
of those who have needs. Give us hearts that are content with knowing
that such giving may be its own reward.
Amen.

DAY 82: PRAYING

*"And whenever you pray, do not be like the hypocrites; for
they love to stand and pray in the synagogues and at the
street corners, so that they may be seen by others. Truly*

I tell you, they have received their reward." (Matthew 6:5, NRSV)

It is possible for a person praying a public prayer to offer encouragement to others. We can encourage each other by praying with each other and before each other as an expression of our common faith and our community identity.

It is possible for a person praying a public prayer to offer edification to others. When someone prays publicly as a way to help others learn how to pray, beneficial education can be shared, particularly when the spirit and attitude of the one leading in prayer is genuine and humble.

But it is also possible, as Jesus points out, for a person praying a public prayer to seek exaltation for herself or for himself. Given the way we are, it is possible for that self-centered motive to be present in us even when our conscious purpose in praying in public is to offer encouragement or edification. Our ego might be seeking exaltation whether or not we set out to do so.

So Lord, teach us to pray. And when we are called upon for any reason to pray in public, remind us that in our prayer we are talking to you and not to anyone else. Remind us that we should be careful how we pray because, even though we are not talking to the others who are present, they are nonetheless listening, and while it is possible that others might somehow benefit from the prayer they hear us pray, we are in no way and at no time to pray so they might hear us and be impressed with our piety or spirituality.

Help us in our praying to want to be—and to be—genuine but not impressive.

Amen.

DAY 83: GOD AND US

"But whenever you pray, go into your room and shut the door and pray to your Father who is in secret; and your Father who sees in secret will reward you. When you are

praying, do not heap up empty phrases as the Gentiles do; for they think that they will be heard because of their many words. Do not be like them, for your Father knows what you need before you ask him." (Matthew 6:6-8, NRSV)

Prayer is, when we get right down to it, conversation and communion between God and us.

Good conversation and communion between two people ordinarily take place best when nobody else is around, so it stands to reason that our best praying will be done with no one else in the room with us but God.

O God, thank you for hearing our prayers. Thank you for your willingness to have the kind of relationship with us that can be developed and deepened through our direct conversation and intimate communion with you.

Forgive us when we settle for something far less with you than you intend for us to have. Forgive us for those days when the only prayers we pray are out of habit or for show.

Help us to find or create environments for our praying that will enhance our speaking to and listening to you.

Thank you for hearing us in secret.

Thank you even more for not being a secret to us.

Amen.

DAY 84: A WAY TO PRAY

"Pray then in this way . . . ." (Matthew 6:9a, NRSV)

On one hand, it would be hard to call wrong any way of praying in which one honestly and openly attempts to commune with God.

On the other hand, Jesus did say that there was a way we should pray, and then he outlined it for us.

Help us, O God, to pray.

Help us, O God, to listen to what Jesus has to say about how we should pray.

Help us, O God, to be open to the spirit of what Jesus says rather than becoming slaves to some prescribed formula for prayer.

Amen.

DAY 85: OUR FATHER

"Our Father . . ." (Matthew 6:9b, NRSV)

O God, we praise you for the wonderful fact that we can pray to you as . . .

   . . . our Father who accepts us,
   . . . our Father who cares for us,
   . . . our Father who holds us,
   . . . our Father who disciplines us,
   . . . our Father who forgives us,
   . . . our Father who nurtures us,
   . . . our Father who carries us,
   . . . our Father who leads us,
   . . . our Father who waits for us,
   . . . our Father who welcomes us,
   . . . our Father who yearns for us,
   . . . our Father who reaches for us, and
   . . . our Father who rescues us.

O God, we praise you for the wonderful fact that we can pray to you as our Father who loves us.

Amen.

DAY 86: IN HEAVEN

"...in heaven..." (Matthew 6:9b, NRSV)

Jesus taught us, on one hand, to pray to God as our Father.

Jesus taught us, on the other hand, to pray to God as our Father who is in heaven.

Whatever else that means, it surely means that in our approaching of God in prayer, we should remember that God is high and lifted up, that God is exalted and holy, and that God is not at our beck and call.

It is God that we approach in prayer, and God should be approached with awe, respect, and reverence.

When we are praying, O God, never let us forget to whom we are talking.

Amen.

DAY 87: HALLOWED BE YOUR NAME

"...hallowed be your name." (Matthew 6:9c, NRSV)

The name of God is the character of God, and God's character is hallowed—is holy and is wholly other—whether we pray that it be hallowed or not.

So to pray this part of the Lord's Prayer is to pray that we will treat the name—the character—of God in light of the facts of who God is and how God is.

Perhaps the primary way that we hallow the name of God is in the way we live. After all, as the children of God we bear the name of God, and as the family of God we bear the likeness of God.

So God, help us live inward and outward lives that treat your name as holy. Help us have thoughts and motives and carry out actions and behaviors that bear witness to who you are in your grace, love, and mercy.

Amen.

DAY 88: YOUR KINGDOM COME

"Your kingdom come..." (Matthew 6:10a, NRSV)

The kingdom of God is the reign or rule of God. There is a sense in which that kingdom is in the future, but there is also a sense in which it is present. The kingdom will be completed when Jesus returns, but it has been right here within us and among us ever since Jesus came.

So . . . come, Lord Jesus.

But also . . . thank you for having come, Lord Jesus.

So . . . may your kingdom be completed and perfected one day, O God.

But also . . . may your kingdom be more completed and perfected in us today and every day, O God.

So . . . may your kingdom be obvious to everybody someday.

But also . . . may your kingdom be obvious in us and through us this day.

Amen.

DAY 89: YOUR WILL BE DONE

"Your will be done..." (Matthew 6:10b, NRSV)

To pray that God's will be done—and mean it—is dangerous.

How, after all, can we voice that prayer and not remember the Lord Jesus voicing it on the night that he was betrayed and arrested? "Father, if it be possible, let this cup pass from me; nevertheless, not my will but your will be done."

How can we forget that he was crucified the next day?

O God, give us grace and courage that we might pray that your will be done—and mean it.

O God, give us grace and courage that we might in faith live into your future regardless of what we have to go through to get there.

O God, give us grace and courage that we might be willing and active partners with you in the doing of your will.

Amen.

DAY 90: ON EARTH

". . . on earth as it is in heaven." (Matthew 6:10c, NRSV)

To pray that God's will be done on earth at it is in heaven raises some interesting—and mind-boggling—possibilities.

After all, don't we assume that God's will is done perfectly in heaven? Don't we assume that the residents of heaven do what God wants them to do?

So if we dare to pray that the Father's will be done on earth as it is done in heaven, aren't we assuming that such doing is possible?

O God, may your will be done on earth as it is in heaven—and we know that one day, when Jesus returns, it will be.

But God, may it be done a little more each day right here and right now in those of us who follow your Son, who call on your name, and who know your grace.

Please open our minds, hearts, spirits, and bodies to the possibilities for our lives, our worship, our witness, our relationships, and our service.

Amen.

DAY 91: OUR DAILY BREAD

"Give us this day our daily bread." (Matthew 6:11, NRSV)

Thank you, God, for this good earth and for the bounty it produces.

Thank you, God, for all of those who do the work needed to provide our food.

Thank you, God, for the ability to labor so we can earn the money we need to purchase food for our families.

And God, help those who get little or no share of that bounty, who have little or no access to the food that is produced, and who don't have the ability or opportunity to earn what they need to feed themselves and their families.

Help us all to do what we can to help those in need.

Help us all to do what we can to change the structures that function in ways that make the distribution of food so inequitable.

Thank you, God, for giving us our daily bread.

Help us, God, to let our thanksgiving compel us to share our bounty. Amen.

DAY 92: FORGIVENESS

"And forgive us our debts, as we also have forgiven our debtors." (Matthew 6:12, NRSV)

Challenge us, O God, with the parables that Jesus told (1) about the Pharisee and the tax collector (Luke 18:9-14) and (2) about the servant who was forgiven an impossible-to-pay-back debt by his master but who would not forgive a small debt owed to him by a peer (Matthew 18:21-35).

Through those parables and through this line of the prayer that Jesus taught us to pray, challenge us with the truth that there is a vital connection between the forgiveness we receive from you and the forgiveness we offer to others as well as between the forgiveness we do not offer to others and the forgiveness we do not receive from you.

Perhaps it all comes down, like so many truths do, to grace. In this case, perhaps the grace we are able to give is a direct reflection of the grace we are able to receive—and vice versa.

Give us, O God, the humility of the tax collector, who would not lift his eyes to heaven but who would only beat his breast and pray, "God, be merciful to me a sinner," that we might truly know and receive your grace.

Give us, O God, an acceptance, appreciation, apprehension, and assimilation of your great grace that grants us such great forgiveness that we can't help but be the opposite of the servant who, despite the great forgiveness he had experienced from his master, still did not have enough grace to share.

Amen.

DAY 93: THE TIME OF TRIAL

"And do not bring us to the time of trial, but rescue us from the evil one." (Matthew 6:13, NRSV)

On one hand, it is best for us to stay out of situations that would test or tempt us. So we pray, "God, keep us out of situations that test or tempt us."

On the other hand, no matter how much we pray to stay out of such situations and no matter how hard we try to stay out of them, sometimes we will find ourselves in them anyway, and so we pray, "God, rescue us from the traps of the evil one."

Jesus seems to indicate that sometimes God leads us into testing, while sometimes the devil ambushes us with temptation. It is hard to escape the thought, though, that often we have quite a lot to do with getting ourselves into the situations that test or tempt us.

That thought seems especially pertinent since Jesus offered this petition between the one that has to do with forgiving others (v. 12) and his further statement about forgiving others (vv. 14-15), the implication being that our greatest tests and temptations have to do with relationships, something at which we are all so flawed.

Beneath the prayer that Jesus taught us to pray lurks another implied prayer, then:

"God, deliver us from ourselves."
Amen.

DAY 94: FORGIVING OTHERS

"For if you forgive others their trespasses, your heavenly Father will also forgive you; but if you do not forgive others, neither will your Father forgive your trespasses." (Matthew 6:14-15, NRSV)

Having been forgiven, we must forgive—and the more we forgive the more forgiveness we are able to receive.

It is how grace works: the more grace we receive, the more grace we will offer; and the more grace we offer, the more grace we will receive.

Rescue us, O God, from a legalism that causes us to think we can earn your forgiveness by forgiving others, for if we think that way, we will spend our lives wondering if the forgiveness we have given is legitimate enough or abundant enough.

But rescue us also, O God, from a shallowness that causes us to think we can receive your free and abundant forgiveness without it causing us, inspiring us, and enabling us to offer our free and abundant forgiveness to others.

Thank you for forgiving us.

Help us develop hearts that by nature dispense so much forgiveness that it opens up room in them to receive more and more forgiveness.

Amen.

DAY 95: FASTING

"And whenever you fast, do not look dismal, like the hypocrites, for they disfigure their faces so as to show others that they are fasting. Truly I tell you, they have received their reward. But when you fast, put oil on your head and wash your face, so that your fasting may be seen not by others but by your Father who is in secret; and your Father who sees in secret will reward you." (Matthew 6:16-17, NRSV)

O God, give us enough grace that we will want to practice basic spiritual disciplines such as fasting and that we will exercise the discipline to do so.

But when we do practice spiritual disciplines such as fasting, help us not to be hypocrites. Help us neither to pretend to be other than we are nor to use the disciplines as a way to demonstrate to others how "holy" we are.

Rescue us from a shallowness that would believe that the pats on the back, the pitying glances, or the jealous looks we would get from others as a result of our "suffering for Jesus" mean anything at all.

The point of spiritual disciplines such as fasting is that they put us in a better position to experience the presence of God. They are, then, between God and us.

Give us grace, O God, to take our relationship with you so seriously that we will be proactive in developing it from our side, inspired by the knowledge that you are always doing so from your side.

Give us faith, O God, to know that you do see and honor our efforts to do what we can to open our lives up to you.

Give us peace, O God, with the knowledge that knowing and being known by you is life's greatest reward.

Amen.

DAY 96: TREASURES

"Do not store up for yourselves treasures on earth, where moth and rust consume and where thieves break in and steal . . . ." (Matthew 6:19, NRSV)

On the one hand, there is a sense in which possessions—basic, necessary possessions—can help define who we are and can thus be important to us; that is why one of the Ten Commandments says we should not steal.

On the other hand, thanks to our tendency to turn good things bad, we too often let our possessions, and especially the pursuit of more and more possessions, rule our lives and determine our priorities.

Jesus teaches us that grasping and hoarding do not befit the character and lifestyle of a disciple; we should have a sound perspective on the gaining and using of possessions because we are not bound by a temporal perspective.

God, help us not to place ultimate value on temporary things; help us not to assign primary significance to secondary things. Show us the lines between saving and hoarding and between having and grasping—and then help us not to cross those lines.

Amen.

DAY 97: TREASURES IN HEAVEN

"But store up for yourselves treasures in heaven, where neither moth nor rust consumes and where thieves do not break in and steal." (Matthew 6:20, NRSV)

Grant, O God, that we will, empowered by your grace and guided by your Spirit, give our constant attention to developing lifestyles that are built on the motives, principles, and relationships that come from you so that we will—here and now—begin to experience the experiences and to be blessed by the blessings that come from you.

Cause us to live even now with an awareness of the eternal life that is ours in Jesus Christ our Lord.

Thank you, God, for the ability to major on majors, for the capability of seeing and living our lives in the context of your kingdom.

Amen.

DAY 98: YOUR TREASURE

"For where your treasure is, there your heart will be also." (Matthew 6:21, NRSV)

Help us, O Lord, to store up our treasures in the right place; help us to store them up in heaven and not on earth.

Forgive us when we give in to self-centeredness and greed that cause us to give our best effort and our greatest energy to building an earthly legacy and to hoarding earthly possessions.

Empower us instead to make you and your will the center of our lives and, as an outgrowth of that proper prioritizing, to put the needs of others ahead of our needs, not to mention our wants.

Take away our pride that causes us to care about how impressed others are with us and with our success, and give us instead humility that causes us to care only about how our thoughts, motives, attitudes, and actions appear in your eyes.

Cause us to have our hearts in the right place. Give us the courage to take a good hard look at where we store up our treasure so that we will know—and, if necessary, do something about—where our hearts are.

Amen.

DAY 99: HEALTHY EYES

"The eye is the lamp of the body. So, if your eye is healthy, your whole body will be full of light; but if your eye is unhealthy, your whole body will be full of darkness. If

then the light in you is darkness, how great is the dark-ness!" (Matthew 6:22-23, NRSV)

Cause us, O God, to be careful about what we let into our lives through our eyes.

Cause us, O God, to be careful about what we set our sights on, about what we make the goal of our lives.

Cause us, O God, to be careful about what we concentrate on, about what we let our eyes dwell on.

Cause us, O God, to be careful about what we look for, about what we make the object of our life's quest.

May what we set our sights on, what we concentrate on, and what we look for lead to our lives being flooded with your light rather than with the world's darkness.

Amen.

DAY 100: TWO MASTERS

"No one can serve two masters; for a slave will either hate the one and love the other, or be devoted to the one and despise the other. You cannot serve God and wealth." (Matthew 6:24, NRSV)

O God, we confess our sin of limping between two opinions, of trying to have it both ways, and of trying to serve two masters.

Forgive us for how we so often try to have you serve our money.

Prod, push, shove, and drive us to have our money serve you.

If we want to know how we regard you, O God, perhaps we need to look at how we regard our money in comparison to how we regard you.

Give us courage to do so honestly.

And then, O God, form our hearts, our lives, and our actions so that it is you we serve—you and you only.

Amen.

DAY 101: MORE THAN

"Therefore I tell you, do not worry about your life, what you will eat or what you will drink, or about your body, what you will wear. Is not life more than food, and the body more than clothing?" (Matthew 6:25, NRSV).

If we trust God to meet our needs ("Give us this day our daily bread"), if we have the right priorities ("Do not store up for yourselves treasures on earth . . . but store up for yourselves treasures in heaven"), and if we serve the right master and don't serve the wrong one ("You cannot serve God and money"), then our anxiety about this life and having adequate provision for it will be considerably lessened.

O God, give us a proper perspective on life and on our physical needs. Help us to live in light of our knowledge that being in relationship with you means having our deepest needs already met.

Lead us to strive for what is "more than" our need to be provided for physically. Lead us not to strive for what is "less than" your grace and love, which are the only human needs whose fulfillment brings a sense of peace, security, and well-being.

Amen.

DAY 102: BIRD-WATCHING

"Look at the birds of the air; they neither sow nor reap nor gather into barns, and yet your heavenly Father feeds them. Are you not of more value than they?" (Matthew 6:26, NRSV)

Help us, Lord, to pay attention to the world around us and to learn from it. Help us to look at the birds of the air and see that you take care of them.

Help us to notice too, Lord, that while "they neither sow nor reap nor gather into barns," the birds nevertheless do what they're supposed to do within the context of what you made them to do. They build nests and find bugs or worms to eat. They flourish by living in the environment in which you made them to live.

Help us, Lord, to live in the environment in which you made us to live, namely, the kingdom of God, so that we too can thrive.

Thank you for feeding us in our bodies. But thank you even more for feeding us in our spirits.

Thank you for feeding us in ways that have temporal value. But thank you even more for feeding us in ways that have eternal value.

Thank you, Lord, that we are of such high value to you that you take such care of us.

Amen.

DAY 103: WORRYING

"And can any of you by worrying add a single hour to your span of life?" (Matthew 6:27, NRSV)

Jesus said that we cannot by worrying add time to our lives. Modern medical science suggests that by worrying, we deduct time from our lives.

Here is one of many cases where the wise thing to do is listen to both Jesus and science.

Lord, we do not pray that you will take away our worrying. To pray that way is only to set ourselves up to worry about why we are still worrying when we have prayed not to worry.

We ask instead, O Lord, that you would fill us with so much trust in you that, over time, worry gets crowded out of our lives.

Amen.

DAY 104: LILY-CONSIDERING

"And why do you worry about clothing? Consider the lilies of the field, how they grow; they neither toil nor spin, yet I tell you, even Solomon in all his glory was not clothed like one of these. But if God so clothes the grass of the field, which is alive today and tomorrow is thrown into the oven, will he not much more clothe you—you of little faith?" (Matthew 6:28-30, NRSV)

Human beings cannot sit around and expect God to drop clothes on our bodies in the same way that God drops beautiful garb on the lilies of the field because, from the beginning, human beings have been meant to work. Adam was put in the garden to till and keep it, after all. He probably took care of some lilies.

Still, God means for us to trust in God. We are to do the best we can do and leave the rest to God.

Since we are of a different character than lilies are—we have spirits, minds, consciences, and relationships—life is going to be more complicated for us than it is for them. Still, we are so much better off if we direct our spirits, minds, consciences, and relationships toward trust in God and away from worry.

O God, help us grow toward having a simple yet mature trust in you that will allow us to conduct our lives with utmost seriousness and, at the same time, leave them in your hands.

Thank you for caring about us. Help us care about each other too, since if we spend our time and energy helping those who struggle to have clothes, we'll spend less time thinking about getting some new ones for ourselves.

Amen.

DAY 105: ENOUGH

"Therefore do not worry, saying, 'What will we eat?' or 'What will we drink?' or 'What will we wear?' For it is the Gentiles who strive for all these things; and indeed your heavenly Father knows that you need all these things." (Matthew 6:31-32, NRSV)

If a person has, like many people in this world, a legitimate lack of decent food to eat, decent water to drink, or decent clothes to wear, then it is perfectly understandable and right that they would ask, "What will we eat?" or "What will we drink?" or "What will we wear?"

The truth is that their heavenly Father has provided enough for them too. But the truth also is that we who have plenty choose to hoard, keep, and grab rather than to offer, give, and share.

Forgive us, Lord, for abusing the grace that gives us enough by not serving as a conduit of your grace to those who don't have enough.

The truth furthermore is that too many of us spend way too much time and energy asking, "What more can I eat?" and "What new variety of drink can I drink?" and "When can I go buy some more clothes for my already overcrowded closet?"

Forgive us, Lord, for committing not the sin of being anxious over having enough but rather for committing the gross sin of being anxious over acquiring more and more and more.

Give us the proper perspective, Lord. Give us the perspective that sees all of our needs, all of our wants, all of our relationships, and all of our responsibilities in the light of the privilege of being your children and in the light of being everyone else's sibling.

Amen.

DAY 106: FIRST

"But strive first for the kingdom of God and his righteousness, and all these things will be given to you as well." (Matthew 6:33, NRSV)

O God, help us grow into striving first for the kingdom of God as we strive for the air we breathe. Help us until we instinctively realize our need for your kingdom. Help us grow into receiving the gift of it.

Show us, O God, that just as going without air will leave us gasping for it, so will going without your kingdom leave us gasping for the peace, the wholeness, the soundness, the relationships, and the meaning that constitute real life.

As long as we have air, all other things pertaining to our physical lives are possible. Help us remember that in a similar way, as long as we are in your kingdom, all other things pertaining not only to our physical lives but also to our spiritual lives will be ours to the degree—and in the proportion—that we need them.

Amen.

DAY 107: TODAY

"So do not worry about tomorrow, for tomorrow will bring worries of its own. Today's trouble is enough for today." (Matthew 6:34, NRSV)

Tomorrow may or may not come for you, and tomorrow may or may not come for me. Worrying about tomorrow, then, is a waste of good effort and energy that could better be used to deal with what the day that has arrived—namely, today—is bringing to us.

The next hour, the next minute, and the next second may or may not come for you or for me. Worrying about even the next moment is a waste of good effort and energy that could be better used to deal with the only reality that we have—namely, the second in which we are alive right now.

Help us, God, not to miss the deep joy or to evade the deep sorrow of this, the only moment in which we are alive, by looking anxiously toward times and events that may or may not arrive.

Give us grace and strength to trust all our moments to you.

Amen.

DAY 108: JUDGING

"Do not judge, so that you may not be judged. For with the judgment you make you will be judged, and the measure you give will be the measure you get." (Matthew 7:1-2, NRSV)

First, O God, please help us not to be so frightened by this teaching of your Son that we are paralyzed into inaction that keeps us from making appropriate progress. After all, who among us would want to be judged by you in the ways that we have judged others? Who would want to receive from you the measure we have given to others?

Second, O God, please help us to grow in grace so that we will not evaluate others by our standards that are limited by our narrow experiences, our narrow spirits, and our narrow vision.

Third, O God, please help us not to be so arrogant as to think that we have enough access to and insight into your standards that we can judge others by them.

Fourth and finally, O God, please help us see others and love others with eyes and hearts that are brimming with grace, mercy, understanding, and compassion—the way your eyes and heart brim when you look at us.

Amen.

DAY 109: SPECKS AND LOGS

"Why do you see the speck in your neighbor's eye, but do not notice the log in your own eye? Or how can you say

to your neighbor, 'Let me take the speck out of your eye,'
while the log is in your own eye? You hypocrite, first take
the log out of your own eye, and then you will see clearly
to take the speck out of your neighbor's eye." (Matthew
7:3-5, NRSV)

You would think that a log in your own eye would get in the way of
seeing a speck in your neighbor's eye—but no.

Human nature, complicated by our sinfulness, allows and even
causes us to perform the amazing feat of ignoring a glaring sin, problem,
discrepancy, or contradiction in our own lives while simultaneously
noticing the smallest sin, problem, discrepancy, or contradiction in
someone else's life.

Forgive us, Lord, for justifying ourselves while we condemn others.

Give us, Lord, the integrity to take a good hard look at who and
how we are so we can seek and accept your grace.

Jesus also teaches that it is possible for his followers to get to a
point of genuine spiritual maturity, a maturity marked by a determined
willingness to become aware of and get rid of their own blatant sin,
hypocrisy, and self-deception so they can legitimately approach a sister
or brother with the goal of helping them deal with some sin that they
are facing.

O God, keep us from trying to approach someone else to "help"
them with their sin when we have not yet faced up to ours.

O God, if we cannot approach a sister or brother with genuine love
and grace and great humility, cause us to keep our "help" to ourselves.

O God, if we can truly see our way clear to try to help someone else,
give us the courageous love required to do so.

And, O God, if we are the ones with a speck in our eye and if we get
a real offer of real help from a real friend, give us the courageous grace
to accept it.

Amen.

DAY 110: PEARLS BEFORE SWINE

"Do not give what is holy to dogs; and do not throw your pearls before swine, or they will trample them under foot and turn and maul you." (Matthew 7:6, NRSV)

Forgive us, O Lord, for our sometimes judgmental attitude that causes us to be overly critical of others and for our sometimes hypocrisy that causes us to hold others to a higher standard than that to which we hold ourselves.

Help us, O Lord, to be so filled with integrity and perspective that we can see our own faults clearly and deal with them appropriately. Help us to be so filled with grace and love that when we see a fault in a sister or brother, our desire for their good compels us to act with compassion and grace.

But there are people—and guard us from concluding this too quickly or too reflexively about any individual or group—who are evil, cruel, abusive, or manipulative, and we need discernment to recognize them and not pretend that they are other than they are. Give us such discernment.

If we must reach such a conclusion about someone, O Lord, remind and motivate us to pray for them. Help us to love them—even if we must do so from a great distance.

Amen.

DAY 111: ASK, SEARCH, KNOCK

"Ask, and it will be given you; search, and you will find; knock, and the door will be opened for you. For everyone who asks receives, and everyone who searches finds, and for everyone who knocks, the door will be opened." (Matthew 7:7-8, NRSV)

Lord, give us hearts that will humbly and honestly ask, search, and knock.

Lord, give us hearts that will lead us to ask for good things.

Lord, give us hearts that will recognize good things when you give them to us.

Amen.

DAY 112: GOOD THINGS

"Is there anyone among you who, if your child asks for bread, will give a stone? Or if the child asks for a fish, will give a snake? If you then, who are evil, know how to give good gifts to your children, how much more will your Father in heaven give good things to those who ask him!" (Matthew 7:9-11, NRSV)

We are unfortunately aware of parents who give bad gifts rather than good gifts and hurtful things rather than helpful things to their children. Lord, work in the hearts, minds, and spirits of such troubled people—both parents and children—that they might find healing and wholeness.

Such awareness notwithstanding, we know that the vast majority of parents are like the ones of whom Jesus speaks. While we are sinners who are too often driven by greed, pride, selfishness, or fear, we would nonetheless never dream of purposely giving our children anything that is not for their good.

Our heavenly Father, Jesus said, is absolutely willing and able to give good things to us when we ask for them.

So God, help us ask for truly good gifts, starting with grace, love, and mercy, and including the ability to follow the instructions for being disciples of Jesus that we find in the Sermon on the Mount.

And help us trust that you will give us those things we need.

Amen.

DAY 113: WANTS

"In everything do to others as you would have them do to you; for this is the law and the prophets." (Matthew 7:12, NRSV)

Dear God,
I want
to be treated fairly,
to be taken seriously,
to be permitted to make mistakes,
to be forgiven,
to be appreciated,
to be encouraged,
to be given credit for what I get right,
to be given some room,
to be accepted,
to be affirmed, and
to be loved.
Help me remember what I want when I am dealing with someone else.
Amen.

DAY 114: THE NARROW GATE

"Enter through the narrow gate; for the gate is wide and the road is easy that leads to destruction, and there are many who take it. For the gate is narrow and the road is hard that leads to life, and there are few who find it." (Matthew 7:13-14, NRSV)

The way that passes through the narrow gate and follows the hard road is the way of Jesus. His way is the way of grace, of trust, of humility, of service, of sacrifice, and of simplicity. It is the way that few take, but it is the way that leads to real life, to a life worth living.

The way that passes through the wide gate and follows the easy road is the way of the world, which is the way of demand, of anxiety, of pride, of greed, of selfishness, and of complication. It is the way that many take, but it is the way that leads to destruction, to a life of futility.

O God, help us take the way of the narrow gate and the hard road rather than the way of the wide gate and the easy road.

And having taken the narrow gate and the hard road, help us not to commit the error of expecting our choice to somehow turn into a wide gate and an easy road. Constantly remind us that the way that leads to life is narrow and hard all the way.

Amen.

DAY 115: FALSE PROPHETS

"Beware of false prophets, who come to you in sheep's clothing but inwardly are ravenous wolves. You will know them by their fruits. Are grapes gathered from thorns, or figs from thistles? In the same way, every good tree bears good fruit, but the bad tree bears bad fruit. A good tree cannot bear bad fruit, nor can a bad tree bear good fruit. Every tree that does not bear good fruit is cut down and thrown into the fire. Thus you will know them by their fruits." (Matthew 7:15-20, NRSV)

Lead us, O Lord, to prophets—to preachers and teachers—who bear fruit that befits leaders who lead in the ways of Jesus because they follow the ways of Jesus.

Help us, O Lord, to look for the right kind of fruit in our preachers and teachers—fruit like grace, faith, mercy, forgiveness, humility, service, sacrifice, peace, and love. Help us follow leaders who show such fruit in their own lives and who help other people produce it in theirs.

Protect us, O Lord, from whatever is in us that will allow us and even cause us to follow leaders who do not lead in the ways of Jesus, who do not produce the fruit that comes from following Jesus, and who lead in ways that are more for their gain than for the good of the kingdom.

As for those of us who are prophets, who are teachers and preachers— Lord, have mercy; Christ, have mercy; Lord, have mercy.

Amen.

DAY 116: LORD, LORD

"Not everyone who says to me, 'Lord, Lord,' will enter the kingdom of heaven, but only the one who does the will of my Father in heaven. On that day many will say to me, 'Lord, Lord, did we not prophesy in your name, and cast out demons in your name, and do many deeds of power in your name?' Then I will declare to them, 'I never knew you; go away from me, you evildoers.'" (Matthew 7:21-23, NRSV)

O God, we acknowledge that right words are not enough. We furthermore acknowledge that the evidence that we belong in the kingdom of heaven is found in our actions and in the motives and attitudes that drive our actions.

Help us, O God, to do your will—to live lives that are fueled by your grace, that are inspired by your love, and that are dedicated to following the teachings and the example of Jesus.

And cause us to know, O God, that to call your name in the right ways and in the right places and with the right people is not enough.

Help us remember that it is possible to do the right things for the wrong reasons with the result that, while our actions may help someone else, they say nothing good about us and may say something bad about us, namely that we are willing to (mis)use the name of Jesus to call attention to ourselves and to gain acclaim for ourselves.

We do know, though, based on the teachings of Jesus, that if our hearts have been touched, changed, and influenced by the grace and love of God, we will be led to do good things, especially to touch the lives of others for good by giving ourselves away with no thought of what we'll get out of it.

We also know, on the other hand, based on the teachings of Jesus, that it is possible to do good things, even the kinds of things that will help other people, but not have those acts motivated by hearts that are full of grace and love.

So God, help us examine our hearts and our actions to see if what is true of us externally is also true of us internally, and vice versa.

May everything about us be the result of your grace and love working in and through us.

May we, in other words, be blessed with integrity.

Amen.

DAY 117: STANDING AND FALLING

"Everyone then who hears these words of mine and acts on them will be like a wise man who built his house on rock. The rain fell, the floods came, and the winds blew and beat on that house, but it did not fall, because it had been founded on rock. And everyone who hears these words of mine and does not act on them will be like a foolish man who built his house on sand. The rain fell, and the floods came, and the winds blew and beat against that house, and it fell—and great was its fall!" (Matthew 7:24-27, NRSV)

God, thank you that in your great grace you sent your Son Jesus to this world to live, to die, and to rise from the grave; thank you also that in your great grace you sent your Son Jesus to this world to share his life and his words with us.

God, help us grasp the truth that his words are the words of life; help us grab hold of them, learn them, and do everything in our power—and more importantly in yours—to follow them.

After all, to fail to do so is to cut ourselves off from the greatest wisdom there is. To fail to do so is to leave ourselves defenseless against the onslaughts of this life.

We want, O God, to make a great stand, not to experience a great fall.

So help us listen to what Jesus says to us . . . and to do it.

Amen.

DAY 118: AUTHORITY

"Now when Jesus had finished saying these things, the crowds were astounded at his teaching, for he taught them as one having authority, and not as their scribes." (Matthew 7:28-29, NRSV)

The difference between the authority of Jesus and that of the scribes was that while Jesus' authority was intrinsic to him, that of the scribes was external to them. Jesus' authority came from who he was, while that of the scribes came from what they knew.

Real authority comes from within, not from without.

Lead us, O God, to listen very, very closely to Jesus. Lead us to take his authority very, very seriously.

Cause our astonishment to give way to obedience. May we follow Christ so closely that our witness comes to flow naturally from within us or, perhaps better put, from our faithful response to your presence in us.

Amen.

DAY 119: JESUS' CHOICE

Now when Jesus had come down from the mountain, large crowds followed him. A man with a skin disease came, kneeled before him, and said, "Lord, if you want, you can make me clean." Jesus reached out his hand

and touched him, saying, "I do want to. Become clean."
Instantly his skin disease was cleansed. (Matthew
8:1-3, CEB)

O Lord,

I think I know what I need. After all, some of my symptoms are
obvious to me, whether or not they are obvious to anyone else.

I also suspect that I need many other types of help and healing
because I suspect that I have infirmities—be they physical, mental,
emotional, social, vocational, or spiritual—of which I am not aware.

So Lord, I ask: please make me clean.

And Lord, I ask: give me faith to accept whatever you choose to
do—or not to do—to me, in me, with me, or through me.

Amen.

DAY 120: SHOWING AND TELLING (OR NOT)

Jesus said to him, "Don't say anything to anyone.
Instead, go and show yourself to the priest and offer the
gift that Moses commanded. This will be a testimony to
them." (Matthew 8:4, CEB)

O God,

We praise you for the wholeness and wellness we experience because
of the grace and love that touch us in Jesus Christ our Lord.

Make us sensitive to the ways in which we should live in our always
developing wholeness and wellness. Give us discernment as to how,
given a particular circumstance or situation, we should bear witness to
others of the healing and help we have found in you.

If we need to tell, lead us to tell. If we need to be silent, lead us to
be silent.

If we need to seek deeper fellowship with the people who share
our faith, lead us to seek that deeper fellowship. If we need to stay to
ourselves for a while, lead us to stay to ourselves.

If we need to go and do, lead us to go and do. If we need to sit and wait, lead us to sit and wait.

As we gratefully accept and embrace your gifts of wholeness and wellness, O God, help us to be sensitive and discerning in our reactions and responses.

Amen.

DAY 121: APPEALING TO JESUS

When Jesus went to Capernaum, a centurion approached, pleading with him, "Lord, my servant is flat on his back at home, paralyzed, and his suffering is awful." Jesus responded, "I'll come and heal him." But the centurion replied, "Lord, I don't deserve to have you come under my roof. Just say the word and my servant will be healed. I'm a man under authority, with soldiers under me. I say to one, 'Go,' and he goes, and to another, 'Come,' and he comes. I say to my servant, 'Do this,' and the servant does it." When Jesus heard this, he was impressed and said to the people following him, "I say to you with all seriousness that even in Israel I haven't found faith like this." (Matthew 8:5-10, CEB)

We appeal to you, Lord, to take care of those about whom we care.

We trust you, Lord, to take care of them according to your mercy and grace.

We accept, O Lord, whatever forms your mercy, grace, care, and curing take.

We thank you, Lord, for hearing and responding to our appeals for the sake of others.

Lord, give us humility that keeps us from expecting more from you than we ought and from behaving as if we somehow have you at our beck and call.

Lord, give us respect that is in awe of your authority and accepts that you can and will accomplish what you want to accomplish in the way you want to accomplish it.

Lord, give us faith that trusts in your grace, in your power, and in your purposes.

Amen.

DAY 122: INSIDERS AND OUTSIDERS

"I say to you that there are many who will come from east and west and sit down to eat with Abraham and Isaac and Jacob in the kingdom of heaven. But the children of the kingdom will be thrown outside into the darkness. People there will be weeping and grinding their teeth." (Matthew 8:11-12, CEB)

Dear Lord,

Grant that we who are the privileged insiders—those who have heard about Jesus and professed to follow Jesus for as long as we can remember—would not take our standing for granted. Help us rather to look to you with great trust and humility.

Grant also that we would not look with disfavor upon those who seem to us to be on the outside. They may well have greater trust and humility than we've ever known.

Keep us from presumption and bless us with trust.

Keep us from arrogance and bless us with humility.

Keep us from exclusiveness and bless us with inclusiveness.

Amen.

DAY 123: SERVING JESUS

When Jesus entered Peter's house, he saw his mother-in-law lying in bed with a fever; he touched her hand,

and the fever left her, and she got up and began to serve him. (Matthew 8:14-15, NRSV)

Thank you, Lord, for the ways you have, by your touch, brought healing and wholeness to us.

Cause us, Lord, to go in that healing and wholeness to serve you in whatever ways we can.

Lead us to celebrate our blessings, not by sitting back and enjoying them, but by going in the strength of them to do whatever we can for you—which almost certainly will mean doing whatever we can for someone else.

Amen.

DAY 124: INFIRMITIES

That evening they brought to him many who were possessed with demons; and he cast out the spirits with a word, and cured all who were sick. This was to fulfill what had been spoken through the prophet Isaiah, "He took our infirmities and bore our diseases." (Matthew 8:16-17, NRSV)

We praise and thank you, O God, that Jesus Christ your Son came to this world to take our infirmities and diseases onto himself, ultimately doing so in his death on the cross.

Help us, O God, as the body of Christ in the world today, to do all we can to help those who are sick and suffering.

Empower us, O God, to share in and to take on their burdens in whatever ways we can, even at great personal cost—all for your glory.

Amen.

DAY 125: THE OTHER SIDE

Now when Jesus saw great crowds around him, he gave orders to go over to the other side. (Matthew 8:18, NRSV)

Lord, fill us with compassion so that we will see the needs in the people around us and then do what we can to help.

But Lord, also give us discernment to know when it is time to get away, for sometimes it is in removing ourselves from a situation that we do the best thing for those around us and for ourselves.

Amen.

DAY 126: WHEREVER

A scribe then approached and said, "Teacher, I will follow you wherever you go." And Jesus said to him, "Foxes have holes, and birds of the air have nests; but the Son of Man has nowhere to lay his head." (Matthew 8:19-20, NRSV)

Lord God, may it be our heart's desire to follow Jesus wherever he leads us.

At the same time, may our commitment to following him be made and carried out with our eyes wide open so we make that commitment with as full an acceptance as possible of what will be expected of us.

Cause and enable us to realize that following Jesus could lead us about anywhere, even to what most people would view as nowhere.

Give us courage to follow anyway, O God.

And give us faith to know that if we are truly trying to follow you, we are following you, and that if we truly want to be where you want us to be, then we are where you want us to be.

Amen.

DAY 127: FIRST THINGS

Another of his disciples said to him, "Lord, first let me go and bury my father." But Jesus said to him, "Follow me, and let the dead bury their own dead." (Matthew 8:21-22, NRSV)

Thank you, God, for the privilege of being disciples of Jesus Christ.

Fill us, God, with the commitment we need to be faithful followers of Jesus Christ.

Remind us, God, that it is in following Jesus Christ that we find real life.

Thank you, God, that ordinarily we can and should express our discipleship and live our lives in ways that allow us to show great care and concern for our families.

Still, God, create in us a sense of true priorities so that there is no doubt in our minds and hearts about who and what come first.

Amen.

DAY 128: ASLEEP

And when he got into the boat, his disciples followed him. A windstorm arose on the sea, so great that the boat was being swamped by the waves; but he was asleep. (Matthew 8:23-24, NRSV)

Lord, we thank you for the gift of sleep that we receive when we are tired.

Lord, we thank you even more for the gift of sleep that we receive because we are at peace.

Help us know that, no matter what comes, we can rest in you.

Help us have the kind of peace that our Savior had, even in the face of the greatest danger.

Amen.

DAY 129: WHY ARE YOU AFRAID?

And they went and woke him up, saying, "Lord, save us! We are perishing!" And he said to them, "Why are you afraid, you of little faith?" Then he got up and rebuked the winds and the sea; and there was a dead calm. They were amazed, saying, "What sort of man is this, that even the winds and the sea obey him?" (Matthew 8:25–27, NRSV)

Lord, sometimes we are afraid. Sometimes we are terrified.

We are afraid because we perceive that we are in danger. Often the danger is imaginary, but sometimes it is very, very real.

Lord, please don't chastise us for our little faith. We are already well aware of how little we have.

Lord, please increase our faith. Help us learn the good and sound lesson of your faithfulness that we know we should have learned long, long ago.

Maybe, Lord, we show a good kind of faith when we trust that you know our predicament whether we tell you about it or not, and when we trust that you will save us whether we ask you to or not.

When the involuntary response of fear comes upon us, Lord, let it be quickly followed by the voluntary reaction of trust in you.

Amen.

DAY 130: THAT WAY

When he came to the other side, to the country of the Gadarenes, two demoniacs coming out of the tombs met him. They were so fierce that no one could pass that way. Suddenly they shouted out, "What have you to do with us, Son of God? Have you come here to torment us before the time?" (Matthew 8:28–29, NRSV)

O God, people and situations confront us that are so dangerous and so disruptive that the sources of the danger and disruption seem beyond the ability of anyone—both perpetrators and targets—to understand.

Sometimes, though, we have to pass that way.

When we do, may the life of Christ be so real and present in us that we contribute to your overcoming of evil with good, to your overcoming of hate with love, and to your overcoming of fear with faith.

Remind us that the time for such overcoming is any time that we are present in this world.

Amen.

DAY 131: DANGER

Now a large herd of swine was feeding at some distance from them. The demons begged him, "If you cast us out, send us into the herd of swine." And he said to them, "Go!" So they came out and entered the swine; and suddenly, the whole herd rushed down the steep bank into the sea and perished in the water. (Matthew 8:30-32, NRSV)

O God, make and keep us mindful of how powerfully damaging and destructive some of the influences are that threaten to control and dominate some of the people around us.

Remind us that some people are struggling in their thinking, feeling, and praying selves with emotional, mental, and spiritual forces that would drive a nonthinking, nonfeeling, and nonpraying being right over a cliff.

Lord, have mercy on them.

Lord, have mercy on us.

Lord, let your mercy flow through us into them.

Amen.

DAY 132: CHALLENGING PRESENCE

The swineherds ran off, and on going into the town, they told the whole story about what had happened to the demoniacs. Then the whole town came out to meet Jesus; and when they saw him, they begged him to leave their neighborhood. (Matthew 8:33-34, NRSV)

Forgive us, O God, when we do not welcome the presence of Jesus among us.

Forgive us when we do not welcome him because he disrupts our status quo.

Forgive us when we do not welcome him because he disrupts our economic systems.

Forgive us especially when we do not welcome him because we'd rather have people remain victimized and ostracized than have to change our ways of looking down on them and refusing to accept them.

Forgive us, O God, when we do not welcome the presence of Jesus among us.

Amen.

DAY 133: HOME

Boarding a boat, Jesus crossed to the other side of the lake and went to his own city. (Matthew 9:1, CEB)

God, by your grace, by our choices, and through circumstances, we live where we live. Sometimes—maybe often—we leave there for short or long times, but we never leave completely, and we usually return.

Thank you for the familiarity of our place. But don't let that familiarity dull our sensitivities to the possibilities of the new and different that are present in it—particularly of the possibilities that reside in the people there, even in those with whom we are most familiar.

Thank you for home.

Help us to do your will—and thereby to do good—there.
Amen.

DAY 134: TAKE HEART

*People brought to him a man who was paralyzed, lying
on a cot. When Jesus saw their faith, he said to the man
who was paralyzed, "Be encouraged, my child, your sins
are forgiven." (Matthew 9:2, CEB)*

Lord, it is easy for us and for others to see what is obviously wrong with
us. It is easy to see our physical problems, social inadequacies, or vocational struggles, for example.

But Lord, it is not so easy for us or for others to see what is not so
obviously wrong with us. It is not easy to see our sin, to see the condition that blocks us from having a life that is full of meaning even in the
midst of outward and obvious struggles.

Lord, thank you for seeing and for doing something about the situation that, when we get right down to it, is our most serious problem.

Thank you that we can take heart, no matter what we are going
through, because our sins are forgiven.

Amen.

DAY 135: THOUGHTS

*Some legal experts said among themselves, "This man is
insulting God." But Jesus knew what they were thinking
and said, "Why do you fill your minds with evil things?"
(Matthew 9:3-4, CEB)*

O God, we acknowledge that you know our every thought.

So when our doubts come—and they do come—grant that they
would be motivated by a true desire to know and to understand rather
than by a desire to dismiss and to avoid.

Grant that we ask our questions about who Jesus is and what Jesus does in a way that will lead

   . . . to greater trust in him rather than to greater doubt about him;

   . . . to greater closeness to him rather than to greater distance from him; and

   . . . to more following of him rather than to more running away from him.

   Amen.

DAY 136: OBVIOUS AND HIDDEN

"Which is easier—to say, 'Your sins are forgiven,' or to say, 'Get up and walk'? But so you will know that the Human One has authority on the earth to forgive sins"—he said to the man who was paralyzed—"Get up, take your cot, and go home." The man got up and went home.
(Matthew 9:5-7, CEB)

Thank you, God, for the occasional glimpses we get that reveal to us in basic and obvious ways your truth about health and wholeness in our lives. Thank you that you use those glimpses to teach and to remind us that you also bring about health and wholeness in ways that are mysterious to us and hidden from us, but that are just as real as the obvious ones.

Deliver us from the small kind of faith that believes only on the basis of the obvious. Grow in us the large kind of faith that believes in what you are doing even when we cannot see it.

Thank you for the ways in which you sometimes heal our outward brokenness. But thank you even more that such healing reminds us that you also heal our inward brokenness, which is the brokenness of which we stand in the greatest need of being healed.

   Amen.

DAY 137: THE CROWDS

When the crowds saw what had happened, they were afraid and praised God, who had given such authority to human beings. (Matthew 9:8, CEB)

O God, we are the Body of Christ, we are the presence of Christ, and we are the hands, feet, and heart of Christ in the world today.

What do the crowds see when they look at us? What is happening in and through us that would cause the crowds to see us and, more important, to see you?

Is our light shining so that others may see it and give glory to our Father in heaven?

Work in and through us, O God, that the suffering of people might be alleviated and that their need for wholeness and healing might be met.

Work in and through us, O God, that we will practice such radical forgiveness and exhibit such radical grace that people will be able to believe in and accept your most radical forgiveness and your most radical grace.

Amen.

DAY 138: CALLED

As Jesus went on from there, He saw a man called Matthew, sitting in the tax collector's booth; and He said to him, "Follow Me!" And he got up and followed Him. (Matthew 9:9, NASB)

In the course of being who he is and doing what he does, Jesus finds us as we are being who we are and doing what we do. It doesn't much matter who we are being and what we are doing, apparently.

The Bible has a lot of accounts of God or Jesus calling people who were going about the business of being good people and doing good things—Noah, Abraham, Deborah, Mary, and Simon Peter, for example.

But the Bible also has a lot of accounts of God or Jesus calling people who were going about the business of being not so good and even bad people and doing not so good and even bad things—Rahab, Samson, Matthew, and Paul, for example.

What does matter is that, in some way or another, when push comes to shove, we get up and follow, and that we then do the best we can.

Lord, we confess that you call us to follow you. We furthermore confess that, whether we are being and doing good or bad or something in between, it is only by your grace that you call us.

Give us trust and strength to get up, to shed our failings and our pretensions, and follow you.

Amen.

DAY 139: SINNERS

Then it happened that as Jesus was reclining at the table in the house, behold, many tax collectors and sinners came and were dining with Jesus and His disciples. (Matthew 9:10, NASB)

Thank you, Lord, that sinners were and are welcome to come and sit with you. Thank you for your hospitality to them. Thank you for your hospitality to us.

Thank you, Lord, that sinners sat at dinner not only with you but also with your disciples, which means that they are welcome to come and sit with those who are your disciples here and now.

The thing is, though, that sometimes we are not as welcoming, not as gracious, and not as loving as we should be. Forgive us and help us.

Another thing is that sometimes our "welcome" is offered in a condescending way. Forgive us and help us.

Grow our spirits so that we will see people as Jesus saw people and that we will love people as Jesus loved people.

Amen.

DAY 140: WHY?

When the Pharisees saw this, they said to His disciples, "Why is your Teacher eating with the tax collectors and sinners?" (Matthew 9:11, NASB)

Because you gave us these minds, O Lord, we ask lots of questions. One we ask quite often is "Why?"

Sometimes "Why?" is a good and necessary question. Sometimes asking it can lead us to new places in our understanding and faith.

Sometimes, though, "Why?" is a misplaced question because behind it lies not a request for information or understanding but rather a need or desire to affirm our assumptions, to bolster our prejudices, or to forward our agenda.

Give us the motivation, O Lord, to ask "Why?" because we want to know and because we are open to new understandings.

Take away the motivation, O Lord, to ask "Why?" because we think we already know and because we want to control or limit our own or someone else's understanding.

Amen.

DAY 141: RIGHT ACTIONS, RIGHT REASONS

But when Jesus heard this, He said, "It is not those who are healthy who need a physician, but those who are sick. But go and learn what this means: 'I desire compassion, and not sacrifice,' for I did not come to call the righteous, but sinners." (Matthew 9:12-13, NASB)

Help us, O God, to do the right things. Help us to respond to people in the right ways because our hearts are moved by the right motives.

Deliver us from substituting association with people of good reputation, who hide their real lives behind their public masks, for friendship with people of questionable reputation, who know who they are and don't try to hide it.

Deliver us from substituting public performance of religious ritual with private involvement in the lives of hurting and searching people.

Deliver us from substituting *looking* like we're doing right and good things for *doing* what you regard as truly right and good things.

Deliver us from hearts that care more about how clean we look than about getting as dirty as we need to get for the sake of love and grace.

Help us, O God, to do the right things; help us, O God, to respond to people in the right ways because our hearts are moved by the right motives.

Amen.

DAY 142: WHY NOT?

Then the disciples of John came to Him, asking, "Why do we and the Pharisees fast, but Your disciples do not fast?" (Matthew 9:14, NASB)

Lord, give us insight into why we as your followers do what we do and don't do what we don't do.

Also, give us patience with those who question why we do what we do and don't do what we don't do.

Furthermore, give us the wisdom to know if and when we need to stop doing something we've been doing or to start doing something we haven't been doing.

Amen.

DAY 143: FASTING AND FEASTING

And Jesus said to them, "The attendants of the bride-groom cannot mourn as long as the bridegroom is with them, can they? But the days will come when the bride-groom is taken away from them, and then they will fast." (Matthew 9:15, NASB)

On one hand, we live on the other side of the crucifixion, so mourning and fasting are appropriate.

On the other hand, we live on the other side of the resurrection, so celebrating and feasting are appropriate.

Sometimes—maybe all the time, in a sense—we mourn and fast because we recognize our lack and our need.

Sometimes—maybe all the time, in a sense—we celebrate and feast because we recognize our abundance and our fulfillment.

Help us, O God, to live in the balance between mourning/fasting and celebrating/feasting that reveals our recognition of both how far we have to go and how far we've come.

Amen.

DAY 144: FRESH WINESKINS

But no one puts a patch of unshrunk cloth on an old garment; for the patch pulls away from the garment, and a worse tear results. Nor do people put new wine into old wineskins; otherwise the wineskins burst, and the wine pours out and the wineskins are ruined; but they put new wine into fresh wineskins, and both are preserved." (Matthew 9:16-17, NASB)

The old ways are generally and usually good.

Sometimes, though, they must be altered or adapted for new circumstances.

And sometimes they must be discarded altogether in favor of something new, particularly something new that our following of Jesus and our listening to the Spirit require.

Give us, O Lord, wisdom and grace to know, from moment to moment, from day to day, and from situation to situation, which approach is required.

Amen.

DAY 145: WITH HIS DISCIPLES

While He was saying these things to them, a synagogue official came and bowed down before Him, and said, "My daughter has just died; but come and lay Your hand on her, and she will live." Jesus got up and began to follow him, and so did His disciples. (Matthew 9:18-19, NASB)

O God, we acknowledge that people still come to and kneel before Jesus Christ, offering up real requests that come from the real love that they have for the real people in their lives. We furthermore acknowledge that, when people come and kneel before Jesus, he still gets up and follows them to the place where the person they love can be found.

And God, we acknowledge that it is still important that we who are the disciples of Jesus get up and go with him to that place of need and to that person in need. Indeed, it may be even more important now, because in these days, we who are the disciples of Jesus are the body of Christ in the world and thus are the channels for the healing and helping power of the Spirit of Christ.

Inspire and compel us to go where Jesus goes. Remind us that he goes to the places where people are in pain and in need.

Amen.

DAY 146: IF I ONLY

And a woman who had been suffering from a hemor-rhage for twelve years, came up behind Him and touched the fringe of His cloak; for she was saying to herself, "If I only touch His garment, I will get well." (Matthew 9:20-21, NASB)

Lord, give us the kind of faith that doesn't need, expect, look for, or demand more than our coming into contact with you.

Give us a heart that needs only a simple, basic relationship with you.

Give us a spirit that expects no more of ourselves than what we can do and no more of you than we should expect.

We are tempted to say,

"If I only move a mountain" or

"If I only have no doubts" or

"If I only commit no sin" or

"If I only am acknowledged as good by everyone" or

"If I only have no more struggles"

or the like.

Give us the kind of faith that can say, "If I only touch his garments"—and mean it.

To come into contact with you, Lord—we affirm that it is enough. Amen.

DAY 147: OUR TRUST

But Jesus turning and seeing her said, "Daughter, take courage; your faith has made you well." At once the woman was made well. (Matthew 9:22, NASB)

We thank you, Lord, that sometimes our trust in you leads to a kind of wholeness and restoration that we and others can see.

But we also thank you, Lord, that sometimes our ability to trust in you regardless of our outward circumstances is in and of itself an important kind of wholeness and restoration, even if the wholeness and restoration happen in inward places that only you—and maybe we—can see.

Thank you for the wholeness and restoration, be it the temporary physical kind or the permanent spiritual kind, that come to us when we put our trust in you.

Amen.

DAY 148: SLEEPING

When Jesus came into the official's house, and saw the flute-players and the crowd in noisy disorder, He said, "Leave; for the girl has not died, but is asleep." And they began laughing at Him. But when the crowd had been sent out, He entered and took her by the hand, and the girl got up. This news spread throughout all that land.
(Matthew 9:23-26, NASB)

O God, sometimes we feel like we're dead or dying—remind us that we're only sleeping.

O God, one day we will die—remind us that we'll only be sleeping.

O God, when we feel like we're dead or dying, take us by the hand so we can get up.

And when we are dead and the great "getting up" morning comes, take us by the hand so we can get up.

Amen.

DAY 149: BLIND

As Jesus went on from there, two blind men followed Him, crying out, "Have mercy on us, Son of David!" When He entered the house, the blind men came up to Him, and Jesus said to them, "Do you believe that I am able to do this?" They said to Him, "Yes, Lord." Then

He touched their eyes, saying, "It shall be done to you according to your faith." And their eyes were opened. (Matthew 9:27-30a, NASB)

Lord, we are blind in any number of ways—blind to our faults, blind to our blessings, blind to our abilities, blind to our sins, blind to our forgiveness, blind to your judgment, blind to your grace.

Lord, we are blind in so many ways.

We believe that you are able to heal our blindness. Please help our unbelief.

Open our eyes, Lord, so we might see what we need to see so we can truly live.

Amen.

DAY 150: SPREADING THE NEWS

And Jesus sternly warned them: "See that no one knows about this!" But they went out and spread the news about Him throughout all that land. (Matthew 9:30b-31, NASB)

Thank you, Lord, for the ways in which you touch us and make us whole. We affirm that when you make us whole, it changes us in ways that can hardly be hidden and in ways that inspire us to, one way or another, make it known to others.

Did these two formerly blind men need to be forgiven for violating your order not to let anyone know that you had healed them? Given that they once were blind but now could see, did you expect them to keep the change a secret? Surely you weren't surprised when they couldn't stop themselves from telling people what you had done for them.

Do we need to be forgiven for *not* spreading the news? Surely you are surprised when we can and do stop ourselves from telling people what you have done for us or don't even think about letting people know what you have done for us. Help us, Lord, not to hide our witness, both in the speaking of words and in the living of life, to who you are and to what you have done in our lives.

Hopefully it shows, whether we are aware of it or not.

Amen.

DAY 151: NEVER BEEN SEEN

As they were going out, a mute, demon-possessed man was brought to Him. After the demon was cast out, the mute man spoke; and the crowds were amazed, and were saying, "Nothing like this has ever been seen in Israel." But the Pharisees were saying, "He casts out the demons by the ruler of the demons." (Matthew 9:32-34, NASB)

Thank you, Lord, for all that we have seen you do in our lives and in the lives of others.

Forgive us for how we take your amazing grace and miraculous love for granted.

Help us to live in grateful acceptance of the ways that you work in us and in others.

Amen.

DAY 152: COMPASSION

Jesus was going through all the cities and villages, teaching in their synagogues and proclaiming the gospel of the kingdom, and healing every kind of disease and every kind of sickness. Seeing the people, He felt compassion for them, because they were distressed and dispirited like sheep without a shepherd. (Matthew 9:35-36, NASB)

The crowds are still with us, O God, and they are still harassed and helpless, like followers without a leader—or at least without a leader who has their best interests at heart.

Help us be so filled with the compassion of Jesus—a compassion that, after all, is making all the difference for us—that we will reach out to the people around us in the ways that we talk, act, and help, even if such talking, acting, and helping is costly to us. And it will be.

Grant that our acts of compassion will always be motivated by compassion and nothing but compassion. Grant that they will never be motivated by selfish motives of seeking status or power.

The crowds are still with us, O God, and they need you. May we be conduits for your compassion.

Amen.

DAY 153: LABORERS

Then He said to His disciples, "The harvest is plentiful, but the workers are few. Therefore beseech the Lord of the harvest to send out workers into His harvest." (Matthew 9:37-38, NASB)

Thank you, Lord, that the physical absence of Jesus from this world does not mean the absence of the body of Christ. Thank you that the church, made up of followers of Jesus Christ, constitutes the body of Christ in the world today.

May we who are the church be filled with your compassion, motivated by your grace, and fueled by your Spirit to be the body of Christ in the world by continuing the ministry of Jesus in preaching, teaching, and helping, so that people who are harassed and helpless might come to know and love you.

In line with Jesus' instructions, we ask that you send the needed laborers out into the world. Whatever the tasks we do and the roles we fill in our daily lives, help us always to know that we are doing your work of offering your compassion and love to everyone we meet.

Amen.

DAY 154: SUMMONED

He called his twelve disciples and gave them authority over unclean spirits to throw them out and to heal every disease and every sickness. Here are the names of the twelve apostles: first, Simon, who is called Peter; and Andrew his brother; James the son of Zebedee; and John his brother; Philip; and Bartholomew; Thomas; and Matthew the tax collector; James the son of Alphaeus; and Thaddaeus; Simon the Cananaean; and Judas, who betrayed Jesus. (Matthew 10:1-4, CEB)

Thank you, Lord, that you call and send your people as a group to do your work and will. Thank you that we are not in this most important work alone.

Thank you also, Lord, that you know, call, and send each of us by name. Thank you that to you, we are not nameless faces in a crowd.

Thank you in addition, Lord, that we have you and that we have each other as we strive to be who we are supposed to be and do what we are supposed to do.

Amen.

DAY 155: INSTRUCTIONS

Jesus sent these twelve out and commanded them, "Don't go among the Gentiles or into a Samaritan city. Go instead to the lost sheep, the people of Israel. As you go, make this announcement: 'The kingdom of heaven has come near.' Heal the sick, raise the dead, cleanse those with skin diseases, and throw out demons." (Matthew 10:5-8a, CEB)

Remind us, O Lord, that instructions tend to be for a particular people in a particular place in a particular time.

So, for example, given that the good news was eventually preached to the Samaritans and the Gentiles, your instructions to the Twelve to go only to the lost sheep of Israel clearly don't apply to us in our time and place. Indeed, they applied to the Twelve only on that particular mission and not on their later mission efforts.

We ask, therefore, for wisdom and discernment in understanding how the instructions given in biblical texts apply to us in our situation. We also ask for wisdom and discernment in understanding the instructions we receive from you in prayer and through the Holy Spirit.

Remind us also, O Lord, that some instructions are given for all your people in all times and in all places. So, for example, even now we are to do what you told the Twelve to do as they went to the people of Israel—we are to carry out ministries of help, healing, and wholeness in your name.

We ask for wisdom and discernment in recognizing the instructions in your Book that are intended for us.

We ask also for the grace and strength not to try to explain them away, but rather to carry them out.

Amen.

DAY 156: ACCEPTANCE AND REJECTION

You received without having to pay. Therefore, give without demanding payment. Workers deserve to be fed, so don't gather gold or silver or copper coins for your money belts to take on your trips. Don't take a backpack for the road or two shirts or sandals or a walking stick. Whatever city or village you go into, find somebody in it who is worthy and stay there until you go on your way. When you go into a house, say, 'Peace!' If the house is worthy, give it your blessing of peace. But if the house isn't worthy, take back your blessing." (Matthew 10:8b-13, CEB)

Grant, Lord, that as we share your grace and love through the living of our lives, we will do so with a spirit of hospitality and blessing.

Help us grow in our receiving of others and in our acceptance of our reception by others.

Help us grow in our assumption that our blessing will be appreciated, well received, and reciprocated.

Help us grow in our desire to partner with others in the sharing of your grace and love.

At the same time, help us grow in our understanding that not everyone will accept us or accept being accepted by us or will bless us or accept being blessed by us. When such refusals happen, grant that they will be directed at us and not practiced by us. When they are directed at us, may we not deserve them due to arrogance, presumption, or pride, and, if we do not invite rejection by our failure to practice Christian grace, give us grace to pray for and to love those who reject us.

Amen.

DAY 157: THE DUST

"If anyone refuses to welcome you or listen to your words, shake the dust off your feet as you leave that house or city. I assure you that it will be more bearable for the land of Sodom and Gomorrah on Judgment Day than it will be for that city." (Matthew 10:14-15, CEB)

Lord, protect us from the pride that can come from the knowledge that we represent you in the world. Give us instead humility and grace.

Lord, protect us from the defensiveness that can come from an expectation that our words will be rejected. Give us instead a realistic hope.

Lord, protect us from the vindictiveness that can come from a too easy assumption that our opponents are your enemies. Give us instead trust in your justice.

Lord, protect us from the belief that in shaking the dust off our feet, we have disconnected ourselves from people. Give us instead a sense that in shaking the dust off our feet, we leave a little of ourselves behind as well.

Amen.

DAY 158: WISE AND INNOCENT

"Look, I'm sending you as sheep among wolves. Therefore, be wise as snakes and innocent as doves." (Matthew 10:16, CEB)

We acknowledge, O God, that the life you have given us is challenging and the mission you have given us is risky. We acknowledge that if we as sheep faithfully follow our shepherd, that if we consistently and intentionally try to live and love as Jesus lived and loved, we will run afoul of the wolves in the world as he did.

So give us sharp and nimble minds that will navigate our way in the world with insight and wisdom.

At the same time, give us hearts that are in the right place—that are in your place—so that we can do what we do and say what we say out of a solid place within us. Give us the motives of grace, service, and selflessness that befit followers of Jesus Christ.

Amen.

DAY 159: TESTIMONY

"Watch out for people—because they will hand you over to councils and they will beat you in their synagogues. They will haul you in front of governors and even kings because of me so that you may give your testimony to them and to the Gentiles." (Matthew 10:17-18, CEB)

Forgive us, Lord, for the carelessness and shallowness that sometimes characterize our faith. Forgive us for thinking and acting as if our lives bear witness to your presence the best when—or only when—we are healthy, wealthy, and well regarded.

Remind us, Lord, that the most meaningful and effective testimony we can offer is a faithfulness that is practiced and a joy that is experienced even when—especially when—we are suffering, poor, and badly regarded . . . or disregarded.

Help us to be a testimony in all circumstances to your presence in us in all circumstances.

Amen.

DAY 160: GIVEN

"Whenever they hand you over, don't worry about how to speak or what you will say, because what you can say will be given to you at that moment. You aren't doing the talking, but the Spirit of my Father is doing the talking through you." (Matthew 10:19-20, CEB)

We praise you, O God, that your Spirit goes with us, speaks to us, and speaks through us.

Help us cultivate such a close relationship with you that not only our words but also our feelings, thoughts, motives, and responses will be guided by your Spirit, not only when we are under stress and pressure but all the time.

Amen.

DAY 161: TO THE END

"Brothers and sisters will hand each other over to be executed. A father will turn his child in. Children will defy their parents and have them executed. Everyone will hate you on account of my name. But whoever

stands firm until the end will be saved. Whenever they harass you in one city, escape to the next, because I assure that you will not go through all the cities of Israel before the Human One comes." (Matthew 10:21-23, CEB)

Lord, strengthen, encourage, and protect your followers for whom being your disciple truly is a divisive, dangerous, and risky reality. Help them to serve you and to bear witness to you in all circumstances. Enable them to endure to the end.

Lord, strengthen, encourage, and protect those of us for whom being your disciple is not a divisive, dangerous, and risky reality. Forgive us for our failure to follow you, which results in a lack of distinctiveness from our culture and keeps us from being misunderstood and mistreated. Help us be faithful enough to risk being driven to ask for your help in enduring to the end.

Strengthen those for whom having the heart to endure to the end is a real issue.

Convict those for whom having the heart to endure to the end is a nonissue.

Amen.

DAY 162: LIKE THE TEACHER

"Disciples aren't greater than their teacher, and slaves aren't greater than their master. It's enough for disciples to be like their teacher and slaves like their master. If they have called the head of the house Beelzebul, it's certain that they will call the members of his household by even worse names." (Matthew 10:24-25, CEB)

Lord, deliver us from a martyr complex that would lead us to want to be maligned. Deliver us also from a persecution complex that would lead us to believe that we are being persecuted whether or not we are.

At the same time, teach us the hard lessons that the road less traveled is not easy street and that going against the current is not a leisurely swim.

Cause us to be true to the ways of Jesus Christ our Lord—the ways of radical grace, love, mercy, peace, faith, hope, and forgiveness. Cause us to be reminded—not morbidly but realistically—of what those ways cost Jesus. Deliver us from a shallowness and foolishness that would let us believe that if we live his life in the world, the people we encounter will accept us better than they did him.

When we pray that we want to be like Jesus, O God, give us clarity as to what we are praying for.

Amen.

DAY 163: CONFIDENT

"Therefore, don't be afraid of those people because nothing is hidden that won't be revealed, and nothing secret that won't be brought out into the open. What I say to you in the darkness, tell in the light; and what you hear whispered, announce from the rooftops. Don't be afraid of those who kill the body but can't kill the soul. Instead, be afraid of the one who can destroy both body and soul in hell. Aren't two sparrows sold for a small coin? But not one of them will fall to the ground without your Father knowing about it already. Even the hairs of your head are all counted. Don't be afraid. You are worth more than many sparrows." (Matthew 10:26-31, CEB)

O God, help us be confident rather than afraid.

Help us be confident in thinking what needs to be thought, in believing what needs to be believed, in saying what needs to be said, and in doing what needs to be done. Help us not to be afraid of thinking, believing, saying, and doing what we must.

Help us be confident in your perspective, mercy, and justice; help us not to be afraid of people's lack of perspective, mercy, and justice.

Help us be confident in your gracious provision and care that extends to us in ways we cannot see and have a hard time even imagining. Help us not to be afraid of personal pain and loss in a way that betrays a lack of trust in your dependable, if mysterious, providence.

O God, help us be confident rather than afraid.

Amen.

DAY 164: ACKNOWLEDGEMENT

"Therefore, everyone who acknowledges me before people, I also will acknowledge before my Father who is in heaven. But everyone who denies me before people, I also will deny before my Father who is in heaven."
(Matthew 10:32-33, CEB)

Since we are joined to Jesus by grace through faith, and since we follow Jesus by grace through faith, O God, help us to acknowledge him—to testify to our real relationship with him—by the ways we talk with, act toward, and treat other people.

May our relationship with Jesus have such legitimacy and such integrity that it is obvious and evident to us, to other people, and to you.

Remind us that it is not so much our words and actions that matter, but the real life and the real relationship that lie behind and motivate our words and actions. Remind us also, though, that if the real life and relationship are there, the words and actions will be too.

Amen.

DAY 165: NOT PEACE

"Don't think that I've come to bring peace to the earth. I haven't come to bring peace but a sword. I've come to turn a man against his father, a daughter against her mother, and a daughter-in-law against her mother-in-law. People's enemies are members of their own households." (Matthew 10:34-36, CEB)

Why is it, O God, that few things in life are more divisive than religion? Why is it that few things in life create more conflict than differences in religious conviction and practice?

We confess the arrogance and presumption that cause us to assume that our way is necessarily better than someone else's way. We acknowledge the simple faith in you that is the life preserver to which we must cling when we begin to wade into deep theological differences and discussions with someone whose perspective is different. Inspire us to offer to share our life preserver with our opponents rather than to try to drown them in the deep waters that could, after all, drown us, too.

At the same time, protect us from foolish thinking that would lead us to believe that other people, even—and maybe especially—those to whom we are closest, will necessarily be pleased at our way of living and will be kindly disposed toward us so that all will be well.

Remind us that it is not necessarily that way. Remind us that the good news of Jesus Christ, with all its love and grace, creates opposition and conflict even within families because, for reasons that are a mystery to us, the good news doesn't sound good to some, and changed lives, even lives that are changed for the better, don't always go over well with those who are used to us being another way, even a much worse way.

But God, if we must encounter opposition from people, even people who are close to us, let it be not because we seek it but rather because it is the inevitable result of a legitimate and humble faith. Please do not let conflict arise because we are pompous, superior, or arrogant in our faith.

Finally, God, please help those people in lands and in situations for whom conflict with families because of their Christian faith is a real, hurtful, and even dangerous situation.

Amen.

DAY 166: LOSING AND FINDING

"Those who love father or mother more than me aren't worthy of me. Those who love son or daughter more than me aren't worthy of me. Those who don't pick up their crosses and follow me aren't worthy of me. Those who find their lives will lose them, and those who lose their lives because of me will find them." (Matthew 10:37-39, CEB)

Help us, Lord, to love you in a way that puts and keeps all our other loves in their proper perspective.

Help us, Lord, to follow Jesus in a way that puts and keeps all our other loyalties in their proper perspective.

Help us, Lord, to live our lives in a way that puts and keeps all of our life in its proper perspective.

Cause us to remember that while loving, following, and living in those ways is costly in the short term, it leads to real and abundant life in the long term.

Amen.

DAY 167: WELCOME

"Those who receive you are also receiving me, and those who receive me are receiving the one who sent me. Those who receive a prophet as a prophet will receive a prophet's reward. Those who receive a righteous person as a righteous person will receive a righteous person's reward. I assure you that everybody who gives even a cup of cold water to these little ones because they are my disciples will certainly be rewarded." (Matthew 10:40-42, CEB)

Lord, we thank you that sometimes we receive help, encouragement, and support from people we know and in ways we can see and acknowledge.

But Lord, we also thank you that sometimes we receive help, encouragement, and support from people we don't know and in ways we can't see or acknowledge.

Lord, give us grace neither to take the first situation for granted nor to be surprised by the second. Give us grace to be grateful for all the help, encouragement, and support we receive as we make this journey of following you.

Amen.

DAY 168: GOING ON

"When Jesus finished teaching his twelve disciples, he went on from there to teach and preach in their cities." (Matthew 11:1, CEB)

Help us, God, to do what Jesus did.

Help us always to focus both on (1) teaching each other and learning from each other so that we can become more effective and mature in our living and serving and (2) going on from there to the people who still need to be introduced to your love and grace.

Protect us from taking an "either/or" approach to ministry. Help us to take a "both/and" approach instead.

Lead us to learn of and from Jesus through prayer, Bible study, and conversations with fellow disciples. Lead us also to take what we learn to people who need to be introduced to the One of and from whom we are learning so much.

Amen.

DAY 169: NO OFFENSE

Now when John heard in prison about the things the Christ was doing, he sent word by his disciples to Jesus, asking, "Are you the one who is to come, or should we look for another?"

Jesus responded, "Go, report to John what you hear and see. Those who were blind are able to see. Those who were crippled are walking. People with skin diseases are cleansed. Those who were deaf now hear. Those who were dead are raised up. The poor have good news proclaimed to them. Happy are those who don't stumble and fall because of me." (Matthew 11:2-6, CEB)

Forgive us, O Lord, when we expect Jesus to be something other than who he is. Forgive us when we expect him to do something other than what he does.

Give us, O Lord, eyes to see the wonderful and amazing gifts of wholeness, meaning, and hope that come to broken people—and we are all broken people—because of who Jesus is and what Jesus does.

Cause us, O Lord, to be true disciples of Jesus who give our time, energy, and resources to accomplishing the same kinds of good that he accomplished and still accomplishes.

Not seeking forgiveness for expecting Jesus to be other than who he is, not seeing the grace he brings to broken people, and not following him by doing what he did—those are all ways that we show we take offense at him.

Lord, have mercy on us.

Amen.

DAY 170: TO SEE

When John's disciples had gone, Jesus spoke to the crowds about John: "What did you go out to the wilderness to see? A stalk blowing in the wind? What did you go out to see? A man dressed up in refined clothes? Look, those who wear refined clothes are in

royal palaces. What did you go out to see? A prophet?
Yes, I tell you, and more than a prophet. He is the one
of whom it is written: 'Look, I'm sending my messenger
before you, who will prepare your way before you.'"
(Matthew 11:7-10, CEB)

O God, if we bear witness to you in the world—and we do, one way or another—people will see us. Cause us to consider what kind of witness we offer to them.

Help us to be strong and even prophetic in our witness. Moreover, help us to be real and authentic in our witness.

More than anything else, though, help us through our witness to prepare the way for others to see you.

Amen.

DAY 171: LEAST

"I assure you that no one who has ever been born is
greater than John the Baptist. Yet whoever is least in the
kingdom of heaven is greater than he. From the days
of John the Baptist until now the kingdom of heaven
is violently attacked as violent people seize it. All the
Prophets and the Law prophesied until John came. If
you are willing to accept it, he is Elijah who is to come.
Let the person who has ears, hear." (Matthew 11:11-15,
CEB)

O Lord, give us grace to be the least in the kingdom of heaven, for it is in weakness, humility, service, and sacrifice that we will be at the center of what you are doing.

O Lord, give us grace to receive our place in the kingdom of heaven as the gift it is, not as something that we must fight for or struggle to achieve.

O Lord, give us grace to know your way in the world and to live your way in the world so we can hear with Christlike ears, think with Christlike minds, talk with Christlike mouths, and act with Christlike motives.

Amen.

DAY 172: THIS GENERATION

"To what will I compare this generation? It is like a child sitting in the marketplaces calling out to others, 'We played the flute for you and you didn't dance. We sang a funeral song and you didn't mourn.' For John came neither eating nor drinking, and they say, 'He has a demon.' Yet the Human One came eating and drinking, and they say, 'Look, a glutton and a drunk, a friend of tax collectors and sinners.' But wisdom is proved to be right by her works." (Matthew 11:16-19, CEB)

Lord, we acknowledge and confess that the kind of life we live can have an impact on the effectiveness of our witness. We furthermore acknowledge and confess that the impact is limited. Sometimes, people are going to hear what they want to hear, see what they want to see, and believe what they want to believe—both about us and about you.

So Lord, make us wise in the ways we live.

But Lord, please soften the hearts, minds, and lives of those around us in this generation, that they might be able to sense and to experience your love and grace. May they even sense them in us.

And Lord, whatever else they say about us and about the ways we live, please let them accuse us of being friends of sinners—and let that accusation be justified!

Amen.

DAY 173: REPENTANCE

Then he began to scold the cities where he had done his greatest miracles because they didn't change their hearts and lives. (Matthew 11:20, CEB)

Cause us, O God, to respond as we should to who Jesus is, to what Jesus says, and to what Jesus has done and still does.

If we need to hear and to accept the reproach of Jesus because we have not acknowledged our waywardness and our lostness, then let us hear and accept his reproach.

Do not let us stay there, though—give us grace truly to repent, truly to let you turn us around and point us in the direction we should go.

Then help us keep walking in that way—in the way of Jesus. Amen.

DAY 174: RESPONDING

"How terrible it will be for you, Chorazin! How terrible it will be for you, Bethsaida! For if the miracles done among you had been done in Tyre and Sidon, they would have changed their hearts and lives and put on funeral clothes and ashes a long time ago. But I say to you that Tyre and Sidon will be better off on Judgment Day than you. And you, Capernaum, will you be honored by being raised up to heaven? No, you will be thrown down to the place of the dead. After all, if the miracles that were done among you had been done in Sodom, it would still be here today. But I say to you that it will be better for the land of Sodom on the Judgment Day than it will be for you." (Matthew 11:21-24, CEB)

Lord, help us accept the great responsibility of responding to your grace that comes with the great privilege of encountering your grace.

And Lord, guard us from the sin of presuming that we have responded to your grace just because we have seen it and heard of it.

Guard us also from the sin of assuming that your grace is so narrow that it applies only to "us" because of who and where we are, or that it is so wide that it applies to "us" whether or not we respond to it and live in it.

Amen.

DAY 175: TO INFANTS

At that time Jesus said, "I praise you, Father, Lord of heaven and earth, because you've hidden these things from the wise and intelligent and have shown them to babies. Indeed, Father, this brings you happiness. "My Father has handed all things over to me. No one knows the Son except the Father. And nobody knows the Father except the Son and anyone to whom the Son wants to reveal him." (Matthew 11:25-27, CEB)

Grant, O Lord, that regardless of our level of intelligence and our attainment of wisdom, we will be open and trusting enough to realize and receive your love and grace.

Let us be smart enough to do some good but not too smart for our own good.

Let it be our heart's desire, O Lord, to be in on the knowing, to be in on the relationship that binds Father and Son and people together.

Let us be people who are humbly aware of our great need, who are much more awed by your grace and love than we are impressed by our wisdom and ability, so that we will be the kind of people to whom the Son chooses to reveal the Father, and who can and will see the One who has been revealed to us.

Thank you, God, that we can trust it all to you.

Help us to do just that.

Amen.

DAY 176: REST

"Come to me, all you who are struggling hard and carrying heavy loads, and I will give you rest. Put on my yoke, and learn from me. I'm gentle and humble. And you will find rest for yourselves. My yoke is easy to bear, and my burden is light." (Matthew 11:28-29, CEB)

Some of us, O Lord, need to wake up to the fact that we carry heavy burdens and that we have weary souls. Indeed, it is those who delude themselves as to the state of their lives—those who claim peace when they have no peace, who claim control where they have no control, who deny their need for grace when all they need is grace—who are in the most trouble.

Pry open the eyes of those of us who have closed ourselves to the state of our lives that we might be able to see the rest that you offer us in Christ Jesus.

Some of us, O Lord, need to wake up to the fact that we choose to continue carrying heavy burdens that you have taken from us and that we choose to continue pursuing wearisome lifestyles when you have given us rest. We still try to be good enough or busy enough or respectable enough, when your grace and what your grace produces is all that can ever be enough.

Pry open the hearts of those of us who have realized our need to come to you for rest but who have not fully accepted it and are not fully living in it.

Your rest is too great a gift to turn down. Help us receive it gladly and fully.

Amen.

DAY 177: NOT LAWFUL

At that time Jesus went through the cornfields on the sabbath; his disciples were hungry, and they began to pluck heads of grain and to eat. When the Pharisees saw

it, they said to him, "Look, your disciples are doing what
is not lawful to do on the sabbath." (Matthew 12:1-2,
NRSV)

Give us, O God, the right perspective on what is right and what is
wrong; give us the right perspective on what is good and what is best;
give us the right perspective on what is harmful and what is helpful.

Help us, O God, to care about and to practice the disciplines of our
faith in ways that will contribute both to our spiritual health and to the
well-being of others.

And help us, O God, to care more about what hungry and hurting
people need than we do about seeing them follow our rules—even if
they are good rules.

Amen.

DAY 178: LORD OF THE SABBATH

He said to them, "Have you not read what David did
when he and his companions were hungry? He entered
the house of God and ate the bread of the Presence,
which it was not lawful for him or his companions to
eat, but only for the priests. Or have you not read in the
law that on the Sabbath the priests in the temple break
the Sabbath and yet are guiltless? I tell you, something
greater than the temple is here. But if you had known
what this means, 'I desire mercy and not sacrifice,' you
would not have condemned the guiltless. For the Son of
Man is lord of the Sabbath." (Matthew 12:3-8, NRSV)

On one hand, O God, keep us from falling into the trap of too easily
justifying doing what we want to do or what others want to do by
pretending that the ancient ways and instructions don't mean anything.

On the other hand, O God, keep us from falling into the trap of too easily concluding that we are righteous and others are not because it appears that we follow the rules and they do not—or of too easily concluding that, because we follow the rules, we have met all of our obligations to you, to ourselves, and to others.

Given that Jesus is our Lord, enable us to view and to treat the traditional spiritual disciplines such as sabbath observance like Jesus viewed and treated them, namely, as disciplines that are worthy of our respect and observance but not as opportunities to condemn other people or neglect our responsibilities toward other people.

O God, help our practice of the spiritual disciplines lead us to practice mercy, fairness, grace, and kindness toward other people.

Amen.

DAY 179: MANIPULATION

He left that place and entered their synagogue; a man was there with a withered hand, and they asked him, "Is it lawful to cure on the Sabbath?" so that they might accuse him. (Matthew 12:9-10, NRSV)

O Lord, please give us grace never to see the plight of another human being as an opportunity to make a point or to support a position.

Guard us from being manipulators.

Please give us grace always to see and to treat people as people.

Amen.

DAY 180: DOING GOOD

He said to them, "Suppose one of you has only one sheep and it falls into a pit on the sabbath; will you not lay hold of it and lift it out? How much more valuable is a human being than a sheep! So it is lawful to do good on the sabbath." Then he said to the man, "Stretch out your hand." He stretched it out, and it was restored, as sound as the other. (Matthew 12:11-13, NRSV)

Cause us, O God, to view other people both as more valuable than the things that are of economic worth to us—some of which we must have—and as more valuable than even our most cherished religious observances—some of which we must observe.

Inspire us, O God, to do good for others in any situation, in any way, and at any time.

Amen.

DAY 181: ALWAYS HELPING

But the Pharisees went out and conspired against him, how to destroy him. When Jesus became aware of this, he departed. Many crowds followed him, and he cured all of them, and he ordered them not to make him known. (Matthew 12:14-16, NRSV)

Give us discernment and wisdom, O God, that we will know when to act publicly and when to act privately, when to confront and when not to confront, and when to speak boldly and when not to speak at all.

But all along the way, O God, regardless of how you lead us to act and to speak, help us do good for all the hurting people we are able to reach.

Amen.

DAY 182: FAITHFUL

This was to fulfill what had been spoken through the prophet Isaiah: "Here is my servant, whom I have chosen, my beloved, with whom my soul is well pleased. I will put my Spirit upon him, and he will proclaim

justice to the Gentiles. He will not wrangle or cry aloud,
nor will anyone hear his voice in the streets. He will not
break a bruised reed or quench a smoldering wick until
he brings justice to victory. And in his name the Gentiles
will hope." (Matthew 12:17-21, NRSV)

Lead us, Lord, to be faithful in bringing hope and justice, in bringing
your good news, to all the people that we are able to reach.

Lead us also, Lord, to be faithful in bringing those needed things to
people in the right ways—the ways Jesus showed us.

Lead us, Lord, to be faithful in living and speaking out of the trust,
the humility, the grace, and the gentleness of the One to whose life and
message we bear witness with our lives and words.

Amen.

DAY 183: CAN THIS BE?

Then they brought to him a demoniac who was blind and
mute; and he cured him, so that the one who had been
mute could speak and see. All the crowds were amazed
and said, "Can this be the Son of David?" (Matthew
12:22-23, NRSV)

Perhaps, O Lord, we ask such a question about Jesus just about every
day: can he be who he appears to be? Can he be who they—who we—
say he is?

Help our thinking be informed by what we see him doing for others
and by what we experience him doing for us.

Then they—and we—just might be the answers to our own
questions.

Amen.

DAY 184: THOUGHTS

But when the Pharisees heard it, they said, "It is only by Beelzebul, the ruler of the demons, that this fellow casts out demons." He knew what they were thinking . . . . (Matthew 12:24-25a, NRSV)

We have our doubts. We have our questions. We have our hesitations.

We have our thoughts.

Sometimes the first thought that jumps into our heads is an accurate thought, but sometimes it is an inaccurate one. Sometimes our first thought is a believing one, but sometimes it is an unbelieving one. Sometimes it is a seeking one, but sometimes it is an avoiding one.

We acknowledge, O Lord, that you know our every thought. Cause that knowledge to lead us not to live in fear but rather to live in trust that you can move us and are moving us to a place of greater faith and hope—if we will let such movement be our goal.

May our thoughts—and your work on, in, and through our thoughts—always contribute to growth in our knowledge of you.

Amen.

DAY 185: MOTIVATION

And said to them, "Every kingdom divided against itself is laid waste, and no city or house divided against itself will stand. If Satan casts out Satan, he is divided against himself; how then will his kingdom stand? If I cast out demons by Beelzebul, by whom do your own exorcists cast them out? Therefore they will be your judges. But if it is by the Spirit of God that I cast out demons, then the kingdom of God has come to you." (Matthew 12:25b-28, NRSV)

We confess, O God, that our motives and purposes, unlike those of Jesus, are not always driven and inspired by doing your will in your way for your reasons. We confess, O God, that we do not always have purity of heart and single-minded purpose.

Please help us grow toward greater Christlikeness in those important areas of life.

Empower us by your Spirit to overcome evil by doing good. May we do so in ways that make it clear that the Spirit who empowers us empowered the actions of Jesus; we are citizens of the kingdom his actions inaugurated.

Amen.

DAY 186: OVERCOMING

"Or how can one enter a strong man's house and plunder his property, without first tying up the strong man? Then indeed the house can be plundered." (Matthew 12:29, NRSV)

Empower us, Lord, to join in your work of tying up the strong man, of limiting the influence and actions of the evil one. Help us live in the ways of Jesus—the ways of love, grace, mercy, and forgiveness—rather than in the ways of the evil one—the ways of hate, legalism, revenge, and unforgiveness.

Empower us, Lord, to join in your work of plundering the strong man's property, of helping people find their way toward the expansive and eternal life that can be theirs in you and away from the limiting and limited life that is theirs in him.

Empower us, Lord, to join in your work of overcoming evil with good.

Amen.

DAY 187: WITH JESUS

"Whoever is not with me is against me, and whoever does not gather with me scatters. Therefore I tell you, people will be forgiven for every sin and blasphemy, but blasphemy against the Spirit will not be forgiven. Whoever speaks a word against the Son of Man will be forgiven, but whoever speaks against the Holy Spirit will not be forgiven, either in this age or in the age to come." (Matthew 12:30-32, NRSV)

Help those of us who follow Jesus, O God, to see what you are doing. Give us discernment to know how you are working in the world to change lives and to set people free. Protect us from refusing to see how the Spirit inspires works of grace and love and from refusing to share in such Spirit-inspired works.

Help those of us who do not follow Jesus, O God, to be led by the Spirit to accept the grace and love of Jesus and his followers, who are being led by the Spirit.

Amen.

DAY 188: ABUNDANCE

"Either make the tree good, and its fruit good; or make the tree bad, and its fruit bad; for the tree is known by its fruit. You brood of vipers! How can you speak good things, when you are evil? For out of the abundance of the heart the mouth speaks. The good person brings good things out of a good treasure, and the evil person brings evil things out of an evil treasure." (Matthew 12:33-35, NRSV)

Lord, guard us from the minor hypocrisy of saying or doing things in an effort to mask who we truly are in our hearts. Protect us from trying to appear to be better than we are.

But Lord, especially guard us from the hypocrisy that results from having deluded ourselves into believing that we are other than what we are. Protect us from thinking that we are better than we are.

Help us see ourselves—our innermost selves—as we truly are. If we are evil, we are evil. If we are good, we are good. But perhaps most of us are somewhere in between or are in some ways both at the same time.

Lord, have mercy! Please move us all more toward you! Please rid our hearts of evil treasure and fill them with good treasure! Please cause us all to be more receptive to your grace! Please let our hearts be so full of you and your love and your grace that what comes out of our mouths and what is done in our lives each day is better and better and healthier and healthier—and has more and more integrity.

Amen.

DAY 189: WORDS

"I tell you, on the day of judgment you will have to give an account for every careless word you utter; for by your words you will be justified, and by your words you will be condemned." (Matthew 12:36-37, NRSV)

We acknowledge, O God, that our words matter more than we usually think they do. Help us take them more seriously, knowing that the content of our words reflects the content of our hearts. That being the case, help us take the content of our hearts with utmost seriousness so we will have a healthy place from which healthy words can and will flow.

Guard us from legalistic paranoia over the silly and meaningless words that we utter in moments of joy, humor, pain, or confusion.

But also guard us from unthinking carelessness about the ways our words, especially our words that reflect on you, on the nature of our relationship with you, and on your ways in the world, can reflect an unthinking carelessness about those most important realities.

Amen.

DAY 190: THE ONLY SIGN

Then some of the scribes and Pharisees said to him, "Teacher, we wish to see a sign from you." But he answered them, "An evil and adulterous generation asks for a sign, but no sign will be given to it except the sign of the prophet Jonah. For just as Jonah was three days and three nights in the belly of the sea monster, so for three days and three nights the Son of Man will be in the heart of the earth. The people of Nineveh will rise up at the judgment with this generation and condemn it, because they repented at the proclamation of Jonah, and see, something greater than Jonah is here! The queen of the South will rise up at the judgment with this generation and condemn it, because she came from the ends of the earth to listen to the wisdom of Solomon, and see, something greater than Solomon is here!" (Matthew 12:38-42, NRSV)

There is not much point, Lord, in trying to get our minds around the sign of the resurrection of Jesus Christ, but if we can get our hearts and spirits wrapped around it—or, maybe better put, if it can get wrapped around our hearts and spirits—well, that makes all the difference.

So help us listen to our resurrected Lord—to his words, to his actions, to the witness of his entire life—more than we listen to anyone else, regardless of how much they merit our attention.

Amen.

DAY 191: BETTER THINGS

"When the unclean spirit has gone out of a person, it wanders through waterless regions looking for a resting place, but it finds none. Then it says, 'I will return to my house from which I came.' When it comes, it finds it

empty, swept, and put in order. Then it goes and brings along seven other spirits more evil than itself, and they enter and live there; and the last state of that person is worse than the first. So will it be also with this evil generation." (Matthew 12:43-45, NRSV)

Help us, O Lord, not to settle for temporary or partial fixes to our spiritual problems. Help us not to settle for seemingly ridding ourselves of what is wrong within us without also welcoming the ways that you will fill us with what is right—with your love, with your grace, and with yourself.

Remind us, O Lord, that right positions, right words, right ideas, and right actions—right as we regard them and even as our community regards them—are not enough, particularly if they consist mainly of what we don't think, don't say, or don't do.

Fill us so much with your life, O Lord, that there is little room for anything else.

Amen.

DAY 192: JESUS' FAMILY

While he was still speaking to the crowds, his mother and his brothers were standing outside, wanting to speak to him. Someone told him, "Look, your mother and your brothers are standing outside, wanting to speak to you." But to the one who had told him this, Jesus replied, "Who is my mother, and who are my brothers?" And pointing to his disciples, he said, "Here are my mother and my brothers! For whoever does the will of my Father in heaven is my brother and sister and mother." (Matthew 12:46-50, NRSV)

O God, it is a difficult and blessed privilege to be members of Jesus' family because it means being disciples of Jesus, which means following him in doing the will of the Father like he did the will of the Father.

And such doing of the Father's will is, the record shows, rewarding in its costliness and costly in its rewards.

Give us strength and grace, O God, to follow Jesus in doing your will. Enable and empower us to love, to give, and to serve as much as we, with your help, possibly can.

Amen.

DAY 193: IN PARABLES

That day Jesus went out of the house and sat down beside the lake. Such large crowds gathered around him that he climbed into a boat and sat down. The whole crowd was standing on the shore. He said many things to them in parables. . . . (Matthew 13:1-3a, CEB)

Inspire us, O Lord, to want to gather around Jesus to hear what he has to teach us.

At the same time, prepare us, O Lord, to deal with the fact that we will not always get straightforward, simple to understand, step-by-step instructions from him.

Parables, after all, are designed to draw us in, to make us part of the story, and to force us to decide.

Prepare us to listen, O Lord.

Also prepare us to think.

Amen.

DAY 194: RECEPTIVE SOIL

"A farmer went out to scatter seed. As he was scattering seed, some fell on the path, and birds came and ate it. Other seed fell on rocky ground where the soil was

shallow. They sprouted immediately because the soil wasn't deep. But when the sun came up, it scorched the plants, and they dried up because they had no roots. Other seed fell among thorny plants. The thorny plants grew and choked them. Other seed fell on good soil and bore fruit, in one case a yield of one hundred to one, in another case a yield of sixty to one, and in another case a yield of thirty to one. Everyone who has ears should pay attention." (Matthew 13:3b-9, CEB)

Lord, only you have the words that can bring us life. By your grace, we ask to find ourselves in a position to hear and receive them so that we can benefit from them for our sake, for the sake of others, and for the sake of your kingdom?

Amen.

DAY 195: GIVEN

Jesus' disciples came and said to him, "Why do you use parables when you speak to the crowds?" Jesus replied, "Because they haven't received the secrets of the kingdom of heaven, but you have. For those who have will receive more and they will have more than enough. But as for those who don't have, even the little they have will be taken away from them." (Matthew 13:10-12, CEB)

If we have been privileged to be given some insight into your way, O Lord, protect us from arrogance that would lead us to think we've seen enough, and grant us humility that always wants to see more.

Remind us that it is not enough for us to settle for what we have already seen.

If we have not yet been given some insight into your way, O Lord, move whatever in us needs to be moved to clear our field of vision so we might see.

Remind us that it is tragic for us to settle for what we haven't seen. Amen.

DAY 196: DULL

"This is why I speak to the crowds in parables: although they see, they don't really see; and although they hear, they don't really hear or understand. What Isaiah prophesied has become completely true for them: You will hear, to be sure, but never understand; and you will certainly see but never recognize what you are seeing. For this people's senses have become calloused, and they've become hard of hearing, and they've shut their eyes so that they won't see with their eyes or hear with their ears or understand with their minds, and change their hearts and lives that I may heal them." (Matthew 13:13-15, CEB)

Help us, O God, to see and admit the factors in our lives that can turn us into people who see but do not perceive, who hear but do not listen, and who have hearts that have grown dull: laziness, disappointment, grief, disillusionment, thoughtlessness, coldness, sorrow, failure, success, and selfishness, just to name a few—any or all of which can lead to a spiritual lifelessness that deprives us of the fullness of life in you that leads to meaning and joy.

If we are people whose dullness and lifelessness cause us to hear your good news in ways that make us become even duller and more lifeless, please intervene by your grace and open our lives up to you.

If we are people whose dullness and lifelessness cause us to hear your good news in ways that cause us to be aware of our dullness and lifelessness, please intervene by your grace and move us more toward you.

If we are people whose dullness and lifelessness were long ago left behind or never in our memory experienced so that we hear your good news in ways that seem to us routine or ordinary, please intervene by your grace and keep our lives open to and amazed by the wonder of it all.

If we are people, O God—and we are—please intervene in our lives by your grace.

Amen.

DAY 197: EYES AND EARS

"Happy are your eyes because they see. Happy are your ears because they hear. I assure you that many prophets and righteous people wanted to see what you see and hear what you hear, but they didn't." (Matthew 13:16-17, CEB)

Thank you, O God, for what—for whom—our eyes have seen and our ears have heard.

Keep us, O God, from ever taking for granted the great blessing of knowing you and of following and learning from Jesus.

Inspire us, O God, to put our experience to good use in the ways we think, talk, and live.

Amen.

DAY 198: THE PENETRATING WORD

"Consider then the parable of the farmer. Whenever people hear the word about the kingdom and don't understand it, the evil one comes and carries off what was planted in their hearts. This is the seed that was sown on the path." (Matthew 13:18-19, CEB)

O God, give all of us—because all of us need your word—the ability not only to hear your word but also to understand it.

May our understanding of it penetrate deep into our hearts and change us so that we know what it is to follow Christ and to be led by your Spirit.

Plant that understanding so deeply in us that neither the evil one nor anyone else has a chance to take it from us.

Amen.

DAY 199: ROOTS

"As for the seed that was spread on rocky ground, this refers to people who hear the word and immediately receive it joyfully. Because they have no roots, they last for only a little while. When they experience distress or abuse because of the word, they immediately fall away." (Matthew 13:20-21, CEB)

Lord, cause your word—the word that we must have if we are to live—to take deep root in our lives.

Cause our initial enthusiasm for your word—as valid, legitimate, and heart-felt as that enthusiasm may be—to give way to a deep and abiding relationship with you that issues in such solid trust that nothing can ever shake it.

Constantly remind us that the way of true joy goes through real trouble. Guard us from a shallowness that is surprised at that reality.

Amen.

DAY 200: FOCUS

"As for the seed that was spread among thorny plants, this refers to those who hear the word, but the worries of this life and the false appeal of wealth choke the word, and it bears no fruit." (Matthew 13:22, CEB)

O God, help us not to allow the cares of the world—the worries, problems, conflicts, and fears—to choke your word in us so that it produces no good fruit.

And God, help us not to allow the lure of wealth—the constant drive to attain more, the temptation to gain more money at any cost, and the focus on seemingly satisfying but ultimately transient things— to choke your word in us so that it produces no good fruit.

And God, help us develop a trust in you that causes us to focus not on the cares of the world but rather on your care for us. Help us follow Jesus so that we focus not on the lure of wealth but rather on the lure of a Christlike life.

Amen.

DAY 201: FRUIT

"As for what was planted on good soil, this refers to those who hear and understand, and bear fruit and produce—in one case a yield of one hundred to one, in another case a yield of sixty to one, and in another case a yield of thirty to one." (Matthew 13:23, CEB)

Lord, cause our lives to be good and fertile soil that is ready to receive the seed of your word. Give us not only ears to hear your word but also minds to understand it and hands and feet to apply it.

May the fruit that our lives bear demonstrate our understanding and incorporation of your word. May it be the kind of fruit that we see in the life of our Lord Jesus Christ.

And give us grace not to compare the amount of fruit—the amount of observable results—that is produced in our lives with that produced in the lives of others. Give us grace to be grateful for whatever you choose to produce through us.

Amen.

DAY 202: WEEDS

Jesus told them another parable: "The kingdom of heaven is like someone who planted good seed in his field. While people were sleeping, an enemy came and planted weeds among the wheat and went away. When the stalks sprouted and bore grain, then the weeds also appeared." (Matthew 13:24-26, CEB)

Help us remember, Lord, that in your kingdom not all the seeds are sown by you, and not all the plants will be good ones. Help us remember that the weeds do come up and that, in some strange way, they may even play their role.

May we who are the wheat learn to coexist peacefully with the weeds.

And may we who are the wheat not, in the ways we relate to the weeds—or to the rest of the wheat, for that matter—appear weedy ourselves.

Amen.

DAY 203: HARVEST TIME

"The servants of the landowner came and said to him, 'Master, didn't you plant good seed in your field? Then how is it that it has weeds?' 'An enemy has done this,' he answered. The servants said to him, 'Do you want us to go and gather them?' But the landowner said, 'No, because if you gather the weeds, you'll pull up the wheat along with them. Let both grow side by side until the harvest. And at harvesttime I'll say to the harvesters, "First gather the weeds and tie them together in bundles to be burned. But bring the wheat into my barn."'" (Matthew 13:27-30, CEB)

We thank you, O God, that the sorting of people—that the determination of who we are and whose we are—is in your hands and not in ours.

We know that you will in every case get it right. We know that we would in many cases get it wrong.

Given the fact that you and only you can make the ultimate determination as to who and whose people we are, guard us, O God, against trying to draw firm conclusions on that subject.

Give us assurance—but not arrogance—about our status. Give us insight—but not judgmentalism—about the status of others.

Amen.

DAY 204: BRANCHES

He told another parable to them: "The kingdom of heaven is like a mustard seed that someone took and planted in his field. It's the smallest of all seeds. But when it's grown, it's the largest of all vegetable plants. It becomes a tree so that the birds in the sky come and nest in its branches." (Matthew 13:31-32, CEB)

Grant, O God, that our local branch of your kingdom will be one in which all sorts of people from all sorts of backgrounds will come and make their home—and will be welcomed by the birds that are already on the branch.

Amen.

DAY 205: YEAST

He told them another parable: "The kingdom of heaven is like yeast, which a woman took and hid in a bushel of wheat flour until the yeast had worked its way through all the dough." (Matthew 13:33, CEB)

Lead and inspire us, O Lord, to embrace our place in the midst of our neighborhood, our town, our nation, and our world so that we can, by living out your grace and love among people, be a positive and creative influence on them.

Amen.

DAY 206: HIDDEN

Jesus said all these things to the crowds in parables, and he spoke to them only in parables. This was to fulfill what the prophet spoke: "I'll speak in parables; I'll declare what has been hidden since the beginning of the world." (Matthew 13:34-35, CEB)

We acknowledge, O God, that Jesus speaks the truth that was previously hidden. We furthermore acknowledge, O God, that Jesus reveals that truth in ways and in words whose understanding requires an insight that comes only by grace through faith.

Open our eyes, hearts, and minds to that grace, to that faith, to that understanding—to that truth.

Amen.

DAY 207: ASSIMILATION

Jesus left the crowds and went into the house. His disciples came to him and said, "Explain to us the parable of the weeds in the field." Jesus replied, "The one who plants the good seed is the Human One. The field is the world. And the good seeds are the followers of the kingdom. But the weeds are the followers of the evil one. The enemy who planted them is the devil. The harvest is the end of the present age. The harvesters are the angels. Just as people gather weeds and burn them in the fire, so it will be at the end of the present age. The Human One will send his angels, and they will gather out of his kingdom all things that cause people to fall away and all people who sin. He will throw them into a burning furnace. People there will be weeping and grinding their teeth. Then the righteous will shine like the sun in their Father's kingdom. Those who have ears should hear." (Matthew 13:36-43, CEB)

Cause the powerful images and symbols employed in the words of your Son, O God, to teach us the important truths to which they point. Prevent us from getting so hung up on the pictures painted that we fail to assimilate the facts being communicated.

Help us assimilate the fact that you are God.

Help us assimilate the fact that history has a purpose and a goal.

Help us assimilate the fact that who we are and who we choose to be matters.

Help us assimilate the fact that the ways we develop or don't develop our lives under you have enduring consequences.

And help us assimilate the fact that since we are still able to assimilate facts, we are still able to have your grace and love shape us so that we become now more of what we can be for all time.

Amen.

DAY 208: EVERYTHING

"The kingdom of heaven is like a treasure that somebody hid in a field, which someone else found and covered up. Full of joy, the finder sold everything and bought that field. Again, the kingdom of heaven is like a merchant in search of fine pearls. When he found one very precious pearl, he went and sold all that he owned and bought it." (Matthew 13:44-45, CEB)

Help us, O Lord, to stay in deep touch with the deep joy that is ours for having found you.

And help us, O Lord, to live in deep awareness of the priceless nature of being known by you and knowing you.

And help us, O Lord, to remain constantly aware of the great value of being in your kingdom, a value so great that we would give up anything and everything—even and especially ourselves—for its sake.

Amen.

DAY 209: SEPARATION

"Again, the kingdom of heaven is like a net that people threw into the lake and gathered all kinds of fish. When it was full, they pulled it to the shore, where they sat down and put the good fish together into containers. But the bad fish they threw away. That's the way it will be at the end of the present age. The angels will go out and separate the evil people from the righteous people, and will throw the evil ones into a burning furnace. People there will be weeping and grinding their teeth."
(Matthew 13:47-50, CEB)

Lord, when we hear these words of Jesus about the separation of people that is to come at the end of the age, we might be filled with relief that justice will one day be done or with sadness that some will choose a way that takes them away from you—or both.

But Lord, if we are counted among the "righteous," cause us to weep and gnash our teeth over the ways that our attitudes, words, and actions might be part of what keeps people from drawing close to you.

Amen.

DAY 210: NEW AND OLD

"Have you understood all these things?" Jesus asked. They said to him, "Yes." Then he said to them, "Therefore, every legal expert who has been trained as a disciple for the kingdom of heaven is like the head of a household who brings old and new things out of their treasure chest." When Jesus finished these parables, he departed. (Matthew 13:51-53, CEB)

Help us understand the life and teachings of Jesus, O God, but guard us against thinking that we have understood all we should or as well as we should.

The ways we feel our feelings, think our thoughts, say our words, and do our deeds will tell the tale.

As we grow in our understanding, O God, cause us to bring together what understanding we have attained in the past and what understanding you give us in the present.

Help us hold on to what has stood the test of time, even as we are open to new ways in which your Spirit might be moving.

Amen.

DAY 211: FAMILIARITY

When he came to his hometown, he taught the people in their synagogue. They were surprised and said, "Where did he get this wisdom? Where did he get the power to work miracles? Isn't he the carpenter's son? Isn't his mother named Mary? Aren't James, Joseph, Simon, and Judas his brothers? And his sisters, aren't they here with us? Where did this man get all this?" They were repulsed by him and fell into sin. But Jesus said to them, "Prophets are honored everywhere except in their own hometowns and in their own households." He was unable to do many miracles there because of their disbelief. (Matthew 13:54-58, CEB)

Protect us, O God, from the presumption that because we know something *about* Jesus, we know Jesus. Protect us from the tendency to close our lives to the gracious power of Jesus because of our presumed familiarity with him.

While it is unlikely that our familiarity with Jesus will breed contempt toward him, do not let it breed carelessness or indifference toward him.

Keep us open to who he is, even as we embrace the mystery and wonder of who he is.

Thank you that we know about Jesus.

Grant that we will know him.

Amen.

DAY 212: CONSCIENCE

At that time Herod the tetrarch heard the news about Jesus, and said to his servants, "This is John the Baptist; he has risen from the dead, and that is why miraculous powers are at work in him." For when Herod had John arrested, he bound him and put him in prison because of Herodias, the wife of his brother Philip. For John had been saying to him, "It is not lawful for you to have her." (Matthew 14:1-4, NASB)

We thank you, Lord, for our consciences, and we ask you to cause them to have a realistic and rational effect on our moral and ethical decisions.

We also ask you to cause a conscience to take root in those who seem to lack one.

May our realization of our sins cause us to repent and to ask for your help in going in a different and better direction. May it not cause us to be so guilt-ridden that we become obsessive and delusional.

Give us a clear and rational acceptance of the way things are with us, and inspire us to seek and to accept your forgiveness. Protect us from refusing forgiveness and from letting our sin and guilt separate us from reality. Remind us that your grace, while unbelievably abundant, is not unbelievable.

Amen.

DAY 213: OATHS

Although Herod wanted to put him to death, he feared the crowd, because they regarded John as a prophet. But when Herod's birthday came, the daughter of Herodias danced before them and pleased Herod, so much that he promised with an oath to give her whatever she asked. Having been prompted by her mother, she said, "Give me here on a platter the head of John the Baptist." Although he was grieved, the king commanded it to be given because of his oaths, and because of his dinner guests. He sent and had John beheaded in the prison. And his head was brought on a platter and given to the girl, and she brought it to her mother. (Matthew 14:5-11, NASB)

We have it in us, O God, to let ourselves get boxed in by what drives us—anger, fear, insecurity, lust, greed, ambition—so that we let ourselves get further boxed in by our words. And in turn, our words commit us to some action that we know, on reflection, would be wrong but one from which, driven by our pride, we won't back down.

So first, O Lord, help us grow so we are driven by positive realities—trust, hope, love, peace, and mercy.

Second, may our words be inspired by those positive realities, but if we are tempted to let them be driven by negative ones, halt our tongues.

Third, if we rashly decide to or state that we will carry out some action that is driven by wrong desires or motives, give us the courage to swallow our pride and to change our minds.

Amen.

DAY 214: LOSS

His disciples came and took away the body and buried it; and they went and reported to Jesus. (Matthew 14:12, NASB)

Sometimes we lose someone or something that means a lot to us.

After the burial, O Lord, help us to remember to tell Jesus about our loss.

In our telling and in his hearing, there is peace, help, and purpose.
Thank you, Lord.
Amen.

DAY 215: GRIEF

Now when Jesus heard this, he withdrew from there in a boat to a deserted place by himself. (Matthew 14:13a)

When John the Baptist died, it was a personal loss to Jesus that also had serious implications for his own life and ministry.

And so he—the Son of God, the Savior of humankind, God's Anointed One—acted on his heartfelt need to be with nothing but his thoughts and prayers and to be with no one but his God.

Remind us, O God, to respond in such healthy ways to our grief, to our losses, and to our challenges.

Remind us, O God, to take time to get away and to be alone.
Amen.

DAY 216: RESPONSE

But when the crowds heard it, they followed him on foot from the towns. When he went ashore, he saw a great

crowd; and he had compassion for them and cured their
sick. (Matthew 14:13b-14, NRSV)

If our ways of thinking, talking, serving, helping, loving—our ways of living—make it obvious that we bear the healing power of your grace and mercy, O Lord, then hurting people will find us wherever we are.

When they find us, we will see them.

When we see them, let our first reaction be compassion.

When we feel compassion, cause us to act on it by offering your help and healing to them in whatever ways we can.

Amen.

DAY 217: RESOURCES

When it was evening, the disciples came to him and said,
"This is a deserted place, and the hour is now late; send
the crowds away so that they may go into the villages
and buy food for themselves." Jesus said to them, "They
need not go away; you give them something to eat."
(Matthew 14:15-16, NRSV)

Our unfortunate tendency, Lord, is to want to send people away when their needs tax our resources—whether our time, energy, money, or love.

Your fortunate tendency, Lord, when we want to send them away, is to challenge us to draw them closer and to dig deep to find the resources we need to help them.

Remind us, Lord, that in you we have a lot more from which to draw than we think we have or are willing to admit we have.

Inspire us, Lord, to rise to your challenge with grace, love, courage, and ingenuity.

Amen.

DAY 218: LEFTOVERS

They replied, "We have nothing here but five loaves and two fish." And he said, "Bring them here to me." Then he ordered the crowds to sit down on the grass. Taking the five loaves and the two fish, he looked up to heaven, and blessed and broke the loaves, and gave them to the disciples, and the disciples gave them to the crowds. And all ate and were filled; and they took up what was left over of the broken pieces, twelve baskets full. (Matthew 14:17-20, NRSV)

Thank you, Lord, that you take what we have—meager though it may be—and that you bless it and break it and give it back to us to give to the people in need who are right in front of us.

Remind us that, if we will trust in your provision for whatever crisis of ministry we face, our next crisis will be to find helpful and creative ways to use all our leftover grace and love.

Amen.

DAY 219: AHEAD

Immediately he made the disciples get into the boat and go on ahead to the other side, while he dismissed the crowds. (Matthew 14:22, NRSV)

On one hand, O God, we know we never go anywhere that Jesus does not go with us. On the other hand, O God, sometimes Jesus compels us to move ahead, to take chances, and to go out in ways that stretch us and that may even seem to put us beyond his reach.

Give us the courage, the trust, the daring—and the memory—that we need to go wherever Jesus sends us, no matter the degree to which the going stretches and challenges us.

Amen.

DAY 220: ALONE

And after he had dismissed the crowds, he went up the mountain by himself to pray. When evening came, he was there alone . . . . (Matthew 14:23, NRSV)

Sometimes, O God, we need to be with other people if we are to be who we are and if we are to be doing what you need us to be doing.

But sometimes, O God, we need to be alone, with no one around except you.

Give us discernment to know which approach is best for the particular time or season of life in which we find ourselves.

Then help us act on the realization to which our discernment leads us.

Amen.

DAY 221: AGAINST

But by this time the boat, battered by the waves, was far from the land, for the wind was against them. (Matthew 14:24, NRSV)

Sometimes out there where we find ourselves, O Lord—at times because we choose to go there, at times because you send us there, and on rare occasions when both realities are happening at the same time—we find ourselves being battered, beaten, and threatened because everything, despite our best intentions and even our best obedience, seems to be working against us.

At those times, O Lord, remind us to look for you, because chances are excellent that you are just beyond the horizon, if not coming right up behind us.

Amen.

DAY 222: DON'T BE AFRAID

And early in the morning he came walking toward them on the sea. But when the disciples saw him walking on the sea, they were terrified, saying, "It is a ghost." And they cried out in fear. But immediately Jesus spoke to them and said, "Take heart, it is I; do not be afraid." (Matthew 14:25-27, NRSV)

Help us, Lord, to be alert for your comings to us, be they in expected and conventional ways or in unexpected and unconventional ways.

Keep us from missing you due to inattention when you come in expected and conventional ways. Shield us from missing you due to confusion when you come in unexpected and unconventional ways.

And regardless of the circumstances out of which or in which you come to us, empty us of fear and fill us with joyful anticipation of and encouragement at your coming.

Amen.

DAY 223: TO JESUS

Peter answered him, "Lord, if it is you, command me to come to you on the water." He said, "Come." So Peter got out of the boat, started walking on the water, and came toward Jesus. (Matthew 14:28-29, NRSV)

Lord, give us courage to ask you to command us to come to you wherever you are.

Lord, give us insight to understand the challenges and risks involved in coming to you wherever you are.

Lord, give us the daring to come to you wherever you are—regardless of how stable or unstable the footing seems to be—because wherever you are is where we belong.

Amen.

DAY 224: CAUGHT

But when [Peter] noticed the strong wind, he became frightened, and beginning to sink, he cried out, "Lord, save me!" Jesus immediately reached out with his hand and caught him, saying to him, "You of little faith, why did you doubt?" (Matthew 14:30-31, NRSV)

Give us such faith, O Lord, that we will keep our eyes on you and keep our trust in you, no matter our situation.

But, given the certainty that we will doubt, Lord, remind us that even as you wonder why we doubt, you still reach out and catch us.

Thank you for your kindness and mercy.

Amen.

DAY 225: TRULY

When they got into the boat, the wind ceased. And those in the boat worshiped him, saying, "Truly you are the Son of God." (Matthew 14:32-33, NRSV)

We thank you, Lord, for the times it is obvious you have removed threats from our lives. In those times, we have the privilege to offer you our whole-hearted praise and worship, since such events make it easy for us to affirm that Jesus is the Son of God.

Grace us with such a deep awareness of and trust in you, though, that we offer such praise and worship to you when events make it necessary for us to affirm that Jesus is the Son of God in spite of the threats that still exist and in times when your deliverance is not so easy for us to discern.

Amen.

DAY 226: BARELY

When they had crossed over, they came to land at Gennesaret. After the people of that place recognized him, they sent word throughout the region and brought all who were sick to him, and begged him that they might touch even the fringe of his cloak; and all who touched it were healed. (Matthew 14:34-36, NRSV)

O God, help us today to be the kinds of friends who bring hurting people to you through prayer, through conversation, and through intervention that they might, even in barely coming into your presence, know wholeness and healing by your grace.

Amen.

DAY 227: TRADITIONS

Then Pharisees and legal experts came to Jesus from Jerusalem and said, "Why are your disciples breaking the elders' rules handed down to us? They don't ritually purify their hands by washing before they eat." (Matthew 15:1-2, CEB)

We thank you, God, for the traditions that have been handed down to us over the years and even over the centuries—and even over the millennia. Help us to respect and to follow them as is appropriate. Help us also to know why we respect and follow them.

And when we decide that we should or must move away from and even discard a tradition, help us to do so because we are led by the spirit, grace, love, and liberty that are ours in Jesus Christ our Lord, and not because we are led by arrogance, contrariness, or novelty.

Amen.

DAY 228: SOUNDNESS

> *Jesus replied, "Why do you break the command of God by keeping the rules handed down to you? For God said, Honor your father and your mother, and The person who speaks against father or mother will certainly be put to death. But you say, 'If you tell your father or mother, "Everything I'm expected to contribute to you I'm giving to God as a gift," then you don't have to honor your father.' So you do away with God's Law for the sake of the rules that have been handed down to you."*
> (Matthew 15:3-6, CEB)

On one hand, O God, we realize that no words on a page, not even those on the pages of the Bible, can be read without being interpreted. It is not possible simply to read and do—so we ask that we will be guided by your Spirit, your grace, and your love in our interpretation and application of your words.

On the other hand, O God, we confess that our interpretation and application of your words is all too often guided instead by our selfishness, our short-sightedness, and our fear.

Grant that we will come to your words with sound motives rather than with unsound ones, so we can understand and live them out in sound ways rather than unsound ones.

Amen.

DAY 229: ATTUNED

> *"Hypocrites! Isaiah really knew what he was talking about when he prophesied about you,' This people honors me with their lips, but their hearts are far away from me. Their worship of me is empty since they teach instructions that are human rules.'"* (Matthew 15:7-9, CEB)

O God, form hearts in us that are attuned to your ways—to your love, grace, and mercy. Give us integrity so the words we offer in worship will reflect that attuning.

Draw our hearts ever closer to you so that our worship, be it offered in the sanctuary or outside it, will be pleasing to you.

Amen.

DAY 230: CORRECTION

Jesus called the crowd near and said to them, "Listen and understand. It's not what goes into the mouth that contaminates a person in God's sight. It's what comes out of the mouth that contaminates the person." Then the disciples came and said to him, "Do you know that the Pharisees were offended by what you just said?" (Matthew 15:10-12, CEB)

Sometimes, Lord, the words that we hear from Jesus, from your Spirit, from your Book, and from those who speak your Word hurt us because they challenge us at the point of our most cherished assumptions about you, about us, about others, and about life.

Give us the maturity to face the fact of our wrongness and of our need for correction. Give us the humility to accept your correction and to assimilate needed positive change in our lives. Give us the perspective to be more concerned with how our words offend you than we are with how your words offend us.

Amen.

DAY 231: LEADERSHIP

Jesus replied, "Every plant that my heavenly Father didn't plant will be pulled up. Leave the Pharisees alone. They are blind people who are guides to blind people. But if a blind person leads another blind person, they will both fall into a ditch." (Matthew 15:13-14, CEB)

As we have need to be led, O God, give us discernment to follow those who have been and are being led by you.

As we have responsibility to lead, O God, help us to lead out of those deep places where we have been and are being led by you.

Amen.

DAY 232: INCREASED UNDERSTANDING

Then Peter spoke up, "Explain this riddle to us." Jesus said, "Don't you understand yet?" (Matthew 15:15-16, CEB)

On one hand, O Lord, it is good for us to ask you for explanations of your teachings that we don't understand. Give us the willingness to do so.

On the other hand, O Lord, it is good for us to hear when you ask why we have not made the progress in our understanding that we should have made. Give us the willingness to do so.

In all circumstances and in every way, O Lord, increase our understanding.

Amen.

DAY 233: THE HEART

"Don't you know that everything that goes into the mouth enters the stomach and goes out into the sewer? But what goes out of the mouth comes from the heart. And that's what contaminates a person in God's sight. Out of the heart come evil thoughts, murders, adultery,

sexual sins, thefts, false testimonies, and insults. These
contaminate a person in God's sight. But eating without
washing hands doesn't contaminate in God's sight."
(Matthew 15:17-20, CEB)

We cannot know for sure, O God, where the things that proceed out of our hearts and defile us come from. We do know for sure, though, that they are there and that they come out in our thoughts, in our motives, in our words, and in our actions.

Lord, have mercy. Cause us to confess, with great realism and honesty, those harmful and destructive attitudes in our hearts, whether they are in the open so that we are aware of them or in hidden corners so that we have to look hard to see them.

And would you please, O God, by your grace and mercy, not only remove them bit by bit but also replace them with positive and helpful attitudes such as good intentions, love, respect, generosity, truth-telling, and affirmation?

Amen.

DAY 234: PLACES

From there, Jesus went to the regions of Tyre and Sidon.
A Canaanite woman from those territories came out and
shouted, "Show me mercy, Son of David. My daughter is
suffering terribly from demon possession." (Matthew
15:21-22, CEB)

Here we are, Lord, where we are, Lord.

There they are, Lord, where they are, Lord.

And you, Lord, are in both places with both groups. You, Lord, are in all places with all groups.

All of us in all of our places will cry out to you because of the great hurts and needs that we and our loved ones have.

Hear our prayer, O Lord: "Lord, have mercy."

Amen.

DAY 235: HUMBLE FAITH

*But he didn't respond to her at all. His disciples came
and urged him, "Send her away; she keeps shouting out
after us." Jesus replied, "I've been sent only to the lost
sheep, the people of Israel." But she knelt before him and
said, "Lord, help me." He replied, "It is not good to take
the children's bread and toss it to dogs." She said, "Yes,
Lord. But even the dogs eat the crumbs that fall off their
masters' table." Jesus answered, "Woman, you have
great faith. It will be just as you wish." And right then
her daughter was healed.* (Matthew 15:23-28, CEB)

O God, keep us from shallow pride that makes us feel entitled to what
we cannot possibly deserve—but what you will nonetheless give us.

O God, teach us the hard lesson of deep humility that leads to deep
trust in your deep grace.

Amen.

DAY 236: WITH

*Jesus moved on from there along the shore of the Galilee
Sea. He went up a mountain and sat down. Large
crowds came to him, including those who were paralyzed, blind, injured, and unable to speak, and many
others. They laid them at his feet, and he healed them.
So the crowd was amazed when they saw those who had
been unable to speak talking, and the paralyzed cured,
and the injured walking, and the blind seeing. And they
praised the God of Israel.* (Matthew 15:29-31, CEB)

As we come before you today, O Lord, do not let us forget to bring
with us those who are hurting, broken, and marginalized. Do not let

us forget to put them at your feet so that you can cure them and make them whole.

Do not let us forget that we come before you best when we do not come before you alone, but rather in the company of those who may need you even more than we do.

In our bringing and in their coming, we and they will find much reason to praise you.

Amen.

DAY 237: AWARENESS

Now Jesus called his disciples and said, "I feel sorry for the crowd because they have been with me for three days and have nothing to eat. I don't want to send them away hungry for fear they won't have enough strength to travel." His disciples replied, "Where are we going to get enough food in this wilderness to satisfy such a big crowd?" (Matthew 15:32-33, CEB)

Fill us with your kind of compassion for the crowd that is with us and around us, Lord—the kind of compassion that cannot bear the thought of sending them away hungry and of thus running the risk that they might, in their weakness and need, not make it all the way home.

Give us an awareness of the resources that we have—resources given to us by you—out of which we might feed them.

At the same time, give us an awareness of the fact that we sometimes are in the desert along with the crowd and so resources are hard to come by. In such times, give us a deep trust in and reliance on you to give us what we need so that we may in turn give it to the hungry people around us.

Fill us with your kind of compassion, Lord, and with the desire and the ingenuity we need to act on it.

Amen.

DAY 238: FILLED

Jesus said, "How much bread do you have?" They responded, "Seven loaves and a few fish." He told the crowd to sit on the ground. He took the seven loaves of bread and the fish. After he gave thanks, he broke them into pieces and gave them to the disciples, and the disciples gave them to the crowds. Everyone ate until they were full. The disciples collected seven baskets full of leftovers. Four thousand men ate, plus women and children. After dismissing the crowds, Jesus got into the boat and came to the region of Magadan. (Matthew 15:34-39, CEB)

We praise you, Lord, for the ways you take what we have, even when it is very little, and do great things with it.

We praise you, Lord, for the ways you involve us in sharing gifts with others.

We praise you, Lord, for the ways people are filled when they receive what we have to offer and what you have blessed and multiplied.

We praise you, Lord, that in our sharing, in your blessing and multiplying, and in their receiving, grace is experienced.

Amen.

DAY 239: THE ONLY SIGN

The Pharisees and Sadducees came up, and testing Jesus, they asked Him to show them a sign from heaven. But He replied to them, "When it is evening, you say, 'It will be fair weather, for the sky is red.' And in the morning, 'There will be a storm today, for the sky is red and threatening.' Do you know how to discern the appearance of the sky, but cannot discern the signs of the times? An evil and adulterous generation seeks after a sign; and a sign will not be given it, except the sign of Jonah." And He left them and went away. (Matthew 16:1-4, NASB)

Give us the kind of faith, O God, that does not ask for any proofs or signs that Jesus is who Jesus is beyond the great sign that has already been given, namely, his resurrection from the dead.

Thank you that we can and do experience Jesus' constant presence with us when we know him in and through his resurrection.

Give us a foundational trust in the only sign that we need and in the only Savior that we need.

Amen.

DAY 240: METAPHORS

And the disciples came to the other side of the sea, but they had forgotten to bring any bread. And Jesus said to them, "Watch out and beware of the leaven of the Pharisees and Sadducees." They began to discuss this among themselves, saying, "He said that because we did not bring any bread." But Jesus, aware of this, said, "You men of little faith, why do you discuss among yourselves that you have no bread?" (Matthew 16:5-8, NASB)

Give us the grace, the insight, the discernment, and the faith, O God, to recognize metaphor and other figurative language when we see it, because sometimes—though not all the time—if we insist on taking your words literally we miss the literal truth that we need to know.

Amen.

DAY 241: MEMORY

"Do you not yet understand or remember the five loaves of the five thousand, and how many baskets full you

picked up? Or the seven loaves of the four thousand, and how many large baskets full you picked up?" (Matthew 16:9-10, NASB)

Forgive us, Lord, for the times when we fail to remember. Forgive us when we fail to remember your mighty acts of the past—not only those we read about in your Book but also those we have experienced in our own lives and in the life of our faith community.

Give us good, active, and perceptive memories, and cause our remembering to contribute to our increasing perception of who you are and to our increasing faith in you.

Help us to learn from our memories of you better to trust in you. Amen.

DAY 242: PERCEPTION

"How is it that you do not understand that I did not speak to you concerning bread? But beware of the leaven of the Pharisees and Sadducees." Then they understood that He did not say to beware of the leaven of bread, but of the teaching of the Pharisees and Sadducees. (Matthew 16:11-12, NASB)

It is so hard to know sometimes, O Lord, to whom we should listen. So many people use so many right-sounding words.

Discernment, Lord—we need discernment.

Wisdom, Lord—we need wisdom.

Insight, Lord—we need insight.

Help us, Lord, to be in tune enough with the Spirit, the love, and the way of Jesus that we can perceive whether the words we are hearing come from someone who is also—maybe even more so—in tune with the Spirit, the love, and the way of Jesus.

Then let our words be similarly worthy of being heard. Amen.

DAY 243: WHO?

Now when Jesus came into the district of Caesarea Philippi, he asked his disciples, "Who do people say that the Son of Man is?" And they said, "Some say John the Baptist, but others Elijah, and still others Jeremiah or one of the prophets." He said to them, "But who do you say that I am?" (Matthew 16:13-15, NRSV)

Help us be aware, O Lord, of the faulty, limited, and just plain wrong ways that many—but certainly not all—people think about you and respond to you.

At the same time, lead us to reflect on the ways that we think about you and respond to you. Help us grow in our understanding of you.

Let our ways of thinking, talking, and acting reveal that we have made much progress in knowing who you truly are.

Amen.

DAY 244: BLESSED

Simon Peter answered, "You are the Messiah, the Son of the living God." And Jesus answered him, "Blessed are you, Simon son of Jonah! For flesh and blood has not revealed this to you, but my Father in heaven. And I tell you, you are Peter, and on this rock I will build my church, and the gates of Hades will not prevail against it." (Matthew 16:16-18, NRSV)

Bless us with the blessing that is ours, O God, when we gain true insight into who Jesus is, insight that is true because it comes from you. Make us open to such truth. Make us willing to embrace and to express such truth.

Help us stand on and live out of our trust in who Jesus is that we might be great contributors to the faithful witness of your church in the world.

Amen.

DAY 245: RESPONSIBILITIES

"I will give you the keys of the kingdom of heaven, and whatever you bind on earth will be bound in heaven, and whatever you loose on earth will be loosed in heaven." Then he sternly ordered the disciples not to tell anyone that he was the Messiah. (Matthew 16:19-20, NRSV)

O God, lead us to acknowledge that our faith in you and our place in your kingdom give us great responsibilities—responsibilities that have to do with the lives, with the faith, and with the pilgrimages of other people.

Give us discipline to take our responsibilities seriously and faith to carry them out with great trust that you will eventually work out the ultimate implications of what we decide and do.

Amen.

DAY 246: DIVINE THINGS

From that time on, Jesus began to show his disciples that he must go to Jerusalem and undergo great suffering at the hands of the elders and chief priests and scribes, and be killed, and on the third day be raised. And Peter took him aside and began to rebuke him, saying, "God forbid it, Lord! This must never happen to you." But he turned and said to Peter, "Get behind me, Satan! You are a stumbling block to me; for you are setting your mind not on divine things but on human things." (Matthew 16:21-23, NRSV)

Given that we live on the other side of the crucifixion, O Lord, it is not possible for us to think or to say that it should not happen or, if we are people of faith, that it did not happen.

It surely is possible, though, for us to live as if it didn't happen. Forbid it, Lord!

Empower us, O Lord, to live lives so full of your grace, love, and Spirit that it is clear that our minds are set on the divine things that Jesus embodied, namely, service and sacrifice. And let it be clear that our minds are set on such divine things because our lives are oriented toward such divine things.

Amen.

DAY 247: FOLLOWERS

Then Jesus told his disciples, "If any want to become my followers, let them deny themselves and take up their cross and follow me. For those who want to save their life will lose it, and those who lose their life for my sake will find it. For what will it profit them if they gain the whole world but forfeit their life? Or what will they give in return for their life?" (Matthew 16:24-26, NRSV)

Remind us, O God, that to be disciples of Jesus is to be students of and followers of Jesus. Remind us that to follow Jesus daily will result in our slowly, consistently, and surely becoming more and more like Jesus.

Remind us furthermore, O God, that Jesus' life was characterized by an utter emptying of himself that was motivated by his obedience to his Father and by his love for us. Remind us that Jesus did not desperately cling to his life but willingly gave it up and thereby found it again.

We want to follow Jesus, O God. We want to deny ourselves and take up our cross and follow him. We want to lose our life for Jesus' sake rather than try to save it for our sake.

See, Lord, we are taking up our cross . . . . See, Lord, we are taking a step . . . .

Amen.

DAY 248: TO COME

"For the Son of Man is to come with his angels in the glory of his Father, and then he will repay everyone for what has been done. Truly I tell you, there are some standing here who will not taste death before they see the Son of Man coming in his kingdom." (Matthew 16:27-28, NRSV)

We trust, O God, in the coming of Jesus to us, however and whenever it happens. We trust in the coming of Jesus to us in his incarnation, in his transfiguration, in his resurrection, and in his second coming, as well as in all of his other comings to us in the ordinary and extraordinary moments and days of our lives.

Whenever and however he comes, O God, grant that we will be found taking up our cross, giving up our lives, and following him.

Amen.

DAY 249: MOUNTAINTOP

Six days later Jesus took with Him Peter and James and John his brother, and led them up on a high mountain by themselves. And He was transfigured before them; and His face shone like the sun, and His garments became as white as light. And behold, Moses and Elijah appeared to them, talking with Him. (Matthew 17:1-3, NASB)

For mountaintop experiences at their best, O God, we thank you. We especially thank you that at their best, our mountaintop experiences give us insight into the nature of our glorified Lord and allow us somehow to enter into his life in a special way so that we might learn how better to live in relationship with him all the time.

We celebrate the fact that Peter, James, and John saw Jesus in his glorified state on that mountain for a short time. We celebrate the fact that not too many days later they saw Jesus in the glorified state that he would have for all time.

And we celebrate the fact that in his resurrection, we too are raised to newness of life. May his glory be reflected in the ways that we think, talk, and live.

Amen.

DAY 250: LISTEN

Peter said to Jesus, "Lord, it is good for us to be here; if You wish, I will make three tabernacles here, one for You, and one for Moses, and one for Elijah." While he was still speaking, a bright cloud overshadowed them, and behold, a voice out of the cloud said, "This is My beloved Son, with whom I am well-pleased; listen to Him!" (Matthew 17:4-5, NASB)

It is good, O God, for us to be in those places and situations in which we experience the grace and love of Jesus in an especially powerful way. We admit our tendency to want to freeze such moments in time rather than to be inspired by them to move forward in our discipleship.

Since by your grace we have been made aware that Jesus is your Beloved Son, cause us to keep listening to him so that, in our consistent following of him, we might find that you are well pleased with us, too.

Amen.

DAY 251: GET UP

When the disciples heard this, they fell face down to the ground and were terrified. And Jesus came to them and touched them and said, "Get up, and do not be afraid." And lifting up their eyes, they saw no one except Jesus Himself alone. (Matthew 17:6-8, NASB)

On one hand, O God, it is natural and appropriate that our reaction to an encounter with you be a reverence so overwhelming that it stops us in our tracks.

On the other hand, O God, it is necessary that we experience the touch of Jesus—the touch that reminds us that you are both the awe-inspiring God of heaven and the gracious God of the incarnation.

Thank you for knocking us down and stopping us in our tracks.

Thank you for helping us back up and putting us back on the path. Amen.

DAY 252: PURPOSE

As they were coming down from the mountain, Jesus commanded them, saying, "Tell the vision to no one until the Son of Man has risen from the dead." And His disciples asked Him, "Why then do the scribes say that Elijah must come first?" And He answered and said, "Elijah is coming and will restore all things; but I say to you that Elijah already came, and they did not recognize him, but did to him whatever they wished. So also the Son of Man is going to suffer at their hands." Then the disciples understood that He had spoken to them about John the Baptist. (Matthew 17:9-13, NASB)

Teach us, Lord, that the ways we presume your purposes should work out are not necessarily the ways your purposes will work out.

But don't allow us to ignore the hard truth that somehow your way is to work your purposes out through the faithful and willing sacrifice of your servants.

Teach us what it means to accept that, in some deep way, the truth for John the Baptist and for Jesus is also the truth for us.

Amen.

DAY 253: COULD NOT

When they came to the crowd, a man met Jesus. He knelt before him, saying, "Lord, show mercy to my son. He is epileptic and suffers terribly, for he often falls into the fire or the water. I brought him to your disciples, but they couldn't heal him." Jesus answered, "You faithless and crooked generation, how long will I be with you? How long will I put up with you? Bring the boy here to me." (Matthew 17:14-17, CEB)

We recognize that the needs of the people around us are great, O Lord.

We recognize also the sense in which, if the people around us are going to come to you for help and healing, they are going to have to come to us, to the church, to the body of Christ.

We furthermore recognize the frustrations that arise both for the people in need and for the church that wants to help them when we are unable to touch them as we need to do.

Give us hearts, O Lord, that want to help. Give us the resources we need to be able to help. Forgive us when our inability to help is because of some shortcoming in us—particularly if it is a shortcoming that is intentionally chosen and selfishly nurtured.

Amen.

DAY 254: TRUST

Then Jesus spoke harshly to the demon. And it came out of the child, who was healed from that time on. Then the disciples came to Jesus in private and said, "Why couldn't we throw the demon out?" "Because you have little faith," he said. "I assure you that if you have faith the size of a mustard seed, you could say to this mountain, 'Go from here to there,' and it will go. There will be nothing that you can't do." (Matthew 17:18-21, CEB)

In the effort to touch hurting people and to heal wounded people, we face situations, problems, and obstacles that seem—and sometimes are—as big as mountains, O God.

For the sake of your kingdom and for the sake of those people, the mountains must be moved, and, since the church is the body of Christ, we must move them.

Give us just a little bit of real trust in you—trust that is born out of our real relationship with you and our real following of you—because just a little bit of real trust in you can help us to move those mountains . . . and nothing else can.

Amen.

DAY 255: DISTRESSED

When the disciples came together in Galilee, Jesus said to them, "The Human One is about to be delivered over into human hands. They will kill him. But he will be raised on the third day." And they were heartbroken. (Matthew 17:22-23, CEB)

We confess, O Lord, that even now we are sometimes distressed by the crucifixion of Jesus.

Cause us to ponder why.

Perhaps we are distressed by the cruelty of those who would harm and kill an innocent person—and by the knowledge that such cruelty still exists today.

Perhaps we are distressed by the realization that someone could be pure of heart enough to give his life for people who don't deserve it—and by the reality that we are among those people.

Perhaps we are distressed by the implications of Jesus' death for those who would dare to be his followers—and by the call on our lives to take up our cross and follow him.

O Lord, take our distress and turn it into inspiration to counter cruelty with love, to counter selfishness with sacrifice, and to counter aimlessness with purpose.

Amen.

DAY 256: FREEDOM

When they came to Capernaum, the people who collected the half-shekel temple tax came to Peter and said, "Doesn't your teacher pay the temple tax?" "Yes," he said. But when they came into the house, Jesus spoke to Peter first." What do you think, Simon? From whom do earthly kings collect taxes, from their children or from strangers?" "From strangers," he said. Jesus said to him, "Then the children don't have to pay. But just so we don't offend them, go to the lake, throw out a fishing line and hook, and take the first fish you catch. When you open its mouth, you will find a shekel coin. Take it and pay the tax for both of us." (Matthew 17:24-27, CEB)

We thank you, God, for the freedom that comes from being your children. We thank you that while we live in the world, we are not bound by the ways of the world or the expectations of the world. We thank you that our citizenship is first and foremost in the kingdom of heaven.

We thank you also, God, for the example of Jesus that inspires us not to use our freedom as an opportunity to run roughshod over the concerns of others who do not share in our freedom.

Teach us not to use our freedom to offend others unnecessarily.
Teach us to use our freedom to be in the world but not of it.
Teach us to use our freedom to love others.
Amen.

DAY 257: LIKE CHILDREN

At that time the disciples came to Jesus and asked, "Who is the greatest in the kingdom of heaven?" He called a child, whom he put among them, and said, "Truly I tell you, unless you change and become like children, you will never enter the kingdom of heaven. Whoever becomes humble like this child is the greatest in the kingdom of heaven. Whoever welcomes one such child in my name welcomes me." (Matthew 18:1-5, NRSV)

Help us, O God, to embrace the truth that the ways of your kingdom are counter to the ways of the world.

Help us, O God, to embrace humility, dependence, vulnerability, and hospitality.

Help us, O God, to embrace the reality that in the mystery of life in Christ, smallness equals greatness.

Help us, O God, to change and become like children.

Help us also welcome those who are like children.

Amen.

DAY 258: STUMBLING BLOCKS

"If any of you put a stumbling block before one of these little ones who believe in me, it would be better for you if a great millstone were fastened around your neck and you were drowned in the depth of the sea. Woe to the world because of stumbling blocks! Occasions for stumbling are bound to come, but woe to the one by whom the stumbling block comes!" (Matthew 18:6-7, NRSV)

We acknowledge, O God, how important it is that we who are adults in the faith, we who have had the privilege of gaining some maturity, take care not to do or say anything that would impede the faith development of those who are children in the faith, who have not yet had the privilege of gaining some maturity. We also acknowledge how important it is for us to live and speak in ways that will help their faith to develop and grow. So help us not to be stumbling blocks to the developing faith of young and new believers. Help us instead to be building blocks.

Amen.

DAY 259: STUMBLING

"If your hand or your foot causes you to stumble, cut it off and throw it away; it is better for you to enter life maimed than to have two hands or two feet and to be thrown into the eternal fire. And if your eye causes you to stumble, tear it out and throw it away; it is better for you to enter life with one eye than to have two eyes and to be thrown into the hell of fire." (Matthew 18:8-9, NRSV)

We confess, O God, that sometimes we stumble, and that in our stumbling we become stumbling blocks for those who are even weaker in their faith than we are.

We acknowledge, O God, the graphic hyperbole of Jesus that makes us aware of how serious such stumbling is.

Please help us receive and grow in the grace that both forgives our stumbling and helps us to grow beyond our stumbling.

Amen.

DAY 260: LOST AND FOUND

"Take care that you do not despise one of these little ones; for, I tell you, in heaven their angels continually see the face of my Father in heaven. What do you think? If a shepherd has a hundred sheep, and one of them has gone astray, does he not leave the ninety-nine on the mountains and go in search of the one that went astray? And if he finds it, truly I tell you, he rejoices over it more than over the ninety-nine that never went astray. So it is not the will of your Father in heaven that one of these little ones should be lost." (Matthew 18:10-14, NRSV)

Help us, Lord, to see those who are struggling with their faith or who are wandering away from you in the same way that you see them—with love, with grace, and with compassion.

Cause us to share in your ruthless pursuit of those who wander away and get lost and to share in your great joy when they are found.

Never let us forget that we are little ones too, and that we can go astray and get lost too, and that we need your love, grace, and compassion—and maybe a little help from our spiritual siblings—too.

Amen.

DAY 261: AGAINST

"If another member of the church sins against you, go and point out the fault when the two of you are alone. If the member listens to you, you have regained that one. But if you are not listened to, take one or two others along with you, so that every word may be confirmed by the evidence of two or three witnesses. If the member refuses to listen to them, tell it to the church; and if the offender refuses to listen even to the church, let such a one be to you as a Gentile and a tax collector." (Matthew 18:15-17, NRSV)

Cause us always to remember, O God, how important our relationships with each other are. Give us the initiative to be proactive in the effort to maintain them when they are whole and to heal them when they are broken.

Give us grace to approach someone who has sinned against us, and give us grace to be approached by someone against whom we have sinned.

Empower your church to be a body within which relationships are valued and real effort to preserve them is expended. And even if a relationship is so badly broken that we have to back away from it, inspire us never to give up on it—just like you never give up on us.

Amen.

DAY 262: AGREE

"Truly I tell you, whatever you bind on earth will be bound in heaven, and whatever you loose on earth will be loosed in heaven. Again, truly I tell you, if two of you agree on earth about anything you ask, it will be done for you by my Father in heaven. For where two or three

are gathered in my name, I am there among them."
(Matthew 18:18-20, NRSV)

Keep us aware, O Lord, of the importance of community and fellowship in your church.

Keep us aware, O Lord, of the responsibility we have to one another and of the accountability we are to have to one another.

Keep us aware, O Lord, of the power that is present through you in the Christian community—power to offer forgiveness, power to offer restoration, power to offer discipline, power to offer acceptance, and power to offer grace.

Keep us aware, O Lord, that we truly are the body of Christ and that you truly are present among us, helping us to help each other grow into the people that we can and should be.

Amen.

DAY 263: SEVENTY-SEVEN

Then Peter came and said to him, "Lord, if another member of the church sins against me, how often should I forgive? As many as seven times?" Jesus said to him, "Not seven times, but, I tell you, seventy-seven times."
(Matthew 18:21-22, NRSV)

Make us so fully and constantly aware of your forgiveness of us, O Lord, that we can't help but have forgiveness flow from us to those who sin against us.

Protect us from a self-congratulatory spirit that is impressed with the forgiveness we are willing and able to offer. Remind us that growing into your kind of forgiveness, growing in having your kind of forgiveness flow through us to others, is a lifelong process, and so we always have the need to make progress.

May the grace that we receive reveal itself in the grace we offer.

Amen.

DAY 264: GRATITUDE

"For this reason the kingdom of heaven may be compared to a king who wished to settle accounts with his slaves. When he began the reckoning, one who owed him ten thousand talents was brought to him; and, as he could not pay, his lord ordered him to be sold, together with his wife and children and all his possessions, and payment to be made. So the slave fell on his knees before him, saying, 'Have patience with me, and I will pay you everything.' And out of pity for him, the lord of that slave released him and forgave him the debt. But that other slave, as he went out, came upon one of his fellow slaves who owed him a hundred denarii; and seizing him by the throat, he said, 'Pay what you owe.' Then his fellow slave fell down and pleaded with him, 'Have patience with me, and I will pay you.' But he refused; then he went and threw him into prison until he would pay the debt." (Matthew 18:23-30, NRSV)

We acknowledge, O God, that we owe you more than we could repay were we to live an infinite number of lifetimes.

We confess our folly in thinking that we could ever by our own effort make things right with you.

But mainly, O God, we praise you for your great compassion that leads you to forgive us. Cause us always to recognize that your great grace is not cheap but is very, very costly to you.

Gratitude, O God—how can we feel anything other than great, great gratitude for your great, great grace?

Grant that your grace would fill us with so much gratitude, O Lord, that it will flow over into the ways that we treat other people.

Grant that your grace would fill us with so much grace, O Lord, that we will forgive others as you have forgiven us.

Amen.

DAY 265: THEY WENT AND REPORTED

"When his fellow slaves saw what had happened, they were greatly distressed, and they went and reported to their lord all that had taken place. Then his lord summoned him and said to him, 'You wicked slave! I forgave you all that debt because you pleaded with me. Should you not have had mercy on your fellow slave, as I had mercy on you?' And in anger his lord handed him over to be tortured until he would pay his entire debt. So my heavenly Father will also do to every one of you, if you do not forgive your brother or sister from your heart." (Matthew 18:31-35, NRSV)

Keep us aware, O God, of our responsibility to one another. Keep us especially alert to those situations in which forgiveness is not appropriately offered and grace is not appropriately practiced in our community of faith.

When we see such actions carried out in our midst, remind us to cry out to you, knowing that you care about the ways your grace does or does not impact our attitudes and behaviors.

Give us the grace to pay enough attention to how other people are mistreated that we will be distressed over it.

And Lord, when we pray the part of the Lord's Prayer that says, "Forgive us our debts as we forgive those who are indebted to us," help us to do so with our eyes wide open.

Constantly remind us of the great mercy you have shown to us, and cause that mercy to flow out constantly from us to the people who have wronged us.

Inspire us by your great forgiveness that comes from your great heart and is thus full and real, Lord, so that our forgiveness will come from our hearts that have been changed and are being changed by your mercy.

Grant that the mercy we extend to others will be as willing and sincere as the mercy you extend to us.

Amen.

DAY 266: WHEREVER

When Jesus finished saying these things, he left Galilee and came to the area of Judea on the east side of the Jordan. Large crowds followed him, and he healed them. (Matthew 19:1-2, CEB)

Wherever we go and wherever we are, O Lord, people will be there. And wherever people are present, so are need and hurt.

So wherever we go, wherever we are, and with whomever we find ourselves, O Lord, position us and empower us to be conduits through which your healing and restoring grace can flow to them.

Amen.

DAY 267: OPENNESS

Some Pharisees came to him. In order to test him, they said, "Does the Law allow a man to divorce his wife for just any reason?" (Matthew 19:3, CEB)

O God, your Book tells us that your Son Jesus has the words of life; we can, therefore, come to him for the help we need as we live these lives of ours.

Help us when we come to him to have minds and hearts that are open to his truth rather than minds and hearts that are looking for ways around his truth.

Give us the grace to seek guidance for the ways he would have us live rather than justification for the ways we want to live.

Amen.

DAY 268: JOINED

Jesus answered, "Haven't you read that at the beginning the creator made them male and female? And God said, 'Because of this a man should leave his father and mother and be joined together with his wife, and the two will be one flesh.' So they are no longer two but one flesh. Therefore, humans must not pull apart what God has put together." (Matthew 19:4-6, CEB)

We praise you, O God, for the gift of personal relationships.

We praise you for the gift of the marriage relationship in which so much mutual fulfillment is possible.

We praise you for the ideal that you established for our marriage relationships. We praise you for the purpose of your creation that is fulfilled in the ways we relate to one another as partners.

Give us grace, O God, to move toward living up to your ideal.

Give us grace, O God, to learn from our failures to live up to your ideal.

Amen.

DAY 269: HARD-HEARTED

The Pharisees said to him, "Then why did Moses command us to give a divorce certificate and divorce her?" Jesus replied, "Moses allowed you to divorce your wives because your hearts are unyielding. But it wasn't that way from the beginning. I say to you that whoever divorces his wife, except for sexual unfaithfulness, and marries another woman commits adultery." His disciples said to him, "If that's the way things are between a man and his wife, then it's better not to marry." He replied, "Not everybody can accept this teaching, but only those who have received the ability to accept it. For there are eunuchs who have been eunuchs from birth. And there are eunuchs who have been made eunuchs by other people. And there are eunuchs who have made themselves eunuchs because of the kingdom of heaven.

Those who can accept it should accept it." (Matthew 19:7-12, CEB)

Make it our hearts' desire, O God, to experience your grace in the best and most positive ways possible.

We recognize and we thank you for the concessions you have made to our humanity and our sinfulness. It is possible, because of your mercy, for us sometimes to justify what we feel like we have had to do even though it did not live up to your best way for us.

And if we did have to do something because it seemed right, even though we knew it was not best, then we thank you for your mercy that allows us to try to keep moving forward.

But please, O God, don't let us take the easy way out. Don't let us nonchalantly tell ourselves that you understand our hard-headedness and our hard-heartedness, and so somehow it's fine for us to do what we want to do.

Fill us instead with the desire to do everything we can, empowered by your love and your Spirit, to live up to the highest ideals possible in our marriage relationships and in all of our relationships.

We thank you for the allowances that your grace sometimes causes you to make, and we ask you for grace that will keep us from needing the allowances quite so much.

Inspire and empower each one of us to live in line with the grace, the insight, and the responsibility with which you have gifted us.

Fill us with your best light and then help us to follow that best light in the living of our lives.

Amen.

DAY 270: CHILDREN

Some people brought children to Jesus so that he would place his hands on them and pray. But the disciples scolded them. "Allow the children to come to me," Jesus said. "Don't forbid them, because the kingdom of heaven belongs to people like these children." Then he blessed

the children and went away from there. (Matthew
19:13-15, CEB)

Prevent us, O Lord, from standing in the way of any who come to you
in their humility, in their need, and in their vulnerability.

Prevent us, O Lord, from standing in our own way of coming to
you by denying our humility, our need, and our vulnerability.

Amen.

DAY 271: WHAT GOOD DEED?

*A man approached him and said, "Teacher, what good
thing must I do to have eternal life?"* (Matthew 19:16,
CEB)

Fill us with the desire, O God, to share in the eternal life that comes
from knowing you.

Guard us from the belief, though, that there is one big thing we can
do to share in that life, as if by our will or by our action we can earn it.

Make and keep us open instead to the truth that we enter into that
life by your grace and that, by your grace, we experience the changes in
our lives that show that we indeed share in eternal life.

Amen.

DAY 272: COMMANDMENTS

*Jesus said, "Why do you ask me about what is good?
There's only one who is good. If you want to enter eternal
life, keep the commandments." The man said, "Which
ones?" Then Jesus said, "Don't commit murder. Don't
commit adultery. Don't steal. Don't give false testimony.*

Honor your father and mother, and love your neighbor as you love yourself." (Matthew 19:17-19, CEB)

It is interesting, O God, that when your Son named the commandments that should be kept if one wishes to experience your real life, he named the "second tablet" commandments—the ones that have to do with how we treat each other.

Somehow, someway, O God, let us take to heart the truth that eternal life involves forgetting self and thinking about others.

Amen.

DAY 273: CONSTANT

The young man replied, "I've kept all these. What am I still missing?" Jesus said, "If you want to be complete, go, sell what you own, and give the money to the poor. Then you will have treasure in heaven. And come follow me." But when the young man heard this, he went away saddened, because he had many possessions. (Matthew 19:20-22, CEB)

O God, give us a constant desire to be moving toward greater wholeness and completeness in this life that we live in you.

Give us a constant awareness of our need for wholeness and completion, an awareness that will not allow us to claim more progress for ourselves than we have made.

Give us a constant willingness to grow in our commitment and ability to give up those things, as you call us to do, that mean the most to us and on which we inappropriately base our security.

Give us a constant motivation to have the life goals of following Jesus and laying up treasure in heaven. Remind us that we do this through service to others and sacrifice for others that are compelled by the presence of your grace in our lives.

Amen.

DAY 274: A RICH PERSON

Then Jesus said to his disciples, "I assure you that it will be very hard for a rich person to enter the kingdom of heaven. In fact, it's easier for a camel to squeeze through the eye of a needle than for a rich person to enter God's kingdom." (Matthew 19:23-24, CEB)

Lord, we confess our inclination to put way too much stock in our stocks—and in our other sources of "security."

As our financial resources stand between us and you, give us the power to let them go.

As they encourage selfishness in us, give us the grace to become selfless with them.

As they lead us to help ourselves, give us the love to help others.

Help us, Lord, to find our security in you and not in our stuff. Amen.

DAY 275: ALL THINGS

When his disciples heard this, they were stunned. "Then who can be saved?" they asked. Jesus looked at them carefully and said, "It's impossible for human beings. But all things are possible for God." (Matthew 19:25-26, CEB)

We ask you, O God, to keep us aware of what we cannot do for ourselves—no matter whatever else we have managed to do for ourselves.

We praise you, O God, that what we cannot do for ourselves, you by your grace and in your love do for us.

Forgive us for our efforts to attempt our impossibilities rather than submitting to and celebrating your possibilities.

It's grace, grace, grace! It's up to you and not up to us—Hallelujah! Amen.

DAY 276: SURPRISES

Then Peter replied, "Look, we've left everything and followed you. What will we have?" Jesus said to them, "I assure you who have followed me that, when everything is made new, when the Human One sits on his magnificent throne, you also will sit on twelve thrones overseeing the twelve tribes of Israel. And all who have left houses, brothers, sisters, father, mother, children, or farms because of my name will receive one hundred times more and will inherit eternal life. But many who are first will be last. And many who are last will be first."
(Matthew 19:27-30, CEB)

First, O God, give us courage to consider the degree to which we are leaving everything and following Jesus.

Second, O God, give us insight to understand that leaving everything and following Jesus is its own reward.

Third, O God, give us grace to look forward to the ongoing and eternal results of our leaving everything and following Jesus.

Fourth, O God, give us humility to remember that when your kingdom fully comes, there will be great surprises in the revealing of who has gone the farthest in leaving everything and following Jesus.

Amen.

DAY 277: DESERVING

[For the full context, read Matthew 20:1-16.] "But he replied to one of them, 'Friend, I am doing you no wrong; did you not agree with me for the usual daily wage? Take what belongs to you and go; I choose to give to this last the same as I give to you. Am I not allowed to do what I choose with what belongs to me? Or are you

envious because I am generous?' So the last will be first,
and the first will be last." (Matthew 20:13-16, NRSV)

Help us, O God, to celebrate wholeheartedly your amazing grace, even
when it is applied to someone else, and especially when it is applied to
someone else who doesn't seem to deserve it—which is, after all, the
point of amazing grace.

Teach us the hard but wonderful lesson that deserving has nothing
to do with grace.

Amen.

DAY 278: UP TO JERUSALEM

While Jesus was going up to Jerusalem, he took the twelve
disciples aside by themselves, and said to them on the
way, "See, we are going up to Jerusalem, and the Son of
Man will be handed over to the chief priests and scribes,
and they will condemn him to death; then they will
hand him over to the Gentiles to be mocked and flogged
and crucified; and on the third day he will be raised."
(Matthew 20:17-19, NRSV)

O God, Jesus said it over and over and we read it over and over and we
hear it over and over: to walk in his way, the way that leads to life, is to
walk in the way of self-emptying service and sacrifice.

To walk in his way is to walk in his truth that leads to his life.

So give us grace and strength to walk in the way of Jesus, wherever
it may lead us.

Amen.

DAY 279: A FAVOR

Then the mother of the sons of Zebedee came to him with her sons, and kneeling before him, she asked a favor of him. And he said to her, "What do you want?" She said to him, "Declare that these two sons of mine will sit, one at your right hand and one at your left, in your kingdom." (Matthew 20:20-21, NRSV)

It is normal and natural, O Lord, that we would ask you to bless our loved ones.

So please bless our loved ones.

Help us, though, to make that request with hearts and minds wide open, accepting that you know not only what is best for our loved ones but also the motives behind our asking.

So do bless their lives.

And do guard our hearts.

Amen.

DAY 280: JESUS' CUP

But Jesus answered, "You do not know what you are asking. Are you able to drink the cup I am about to drink?" They said to him, "We are able." He said to them, "You will indeed drink my cup, but to sit at my right hand and at my left, this is not mine to grant, but it is for those for whom it has been prepared by my Father." (Matthew 20:22-23, NRSV)

Teach us, O Lord, what it means to drink your cup. Teach us that it means to share in your life, which in turn means to share in your service, in your sacrifice, and in your suffering.

Guard us from arrogant thoughtlessness that would lead us to make claims of an ability to drink your cup that we do not possess.

Guard us from timid reticence that would lead us to shrink from a humble willingness to at least be always moving toward an ability to drink your cup.

Guard us from selfish seeking that would lead us to draw the inspiration for our willingness to drink your cup from the hope of reward for doing so.

Give us, O Lord, minds, hearts, and spirits like yours so we will want to drink your cup, to share in your life, which in turn means to share in your service, in your sacrifice, and in your suffering—because it is what we truly want to do.

Amen.

DAY 281: SERVING AND GIVING

When the ten heard it, they were angry with the two brothers. But Jesus called them to him and said, "You know that the rulers of the Gentiles lord it over them, and their great ones are tyrants over them. It will not be so among you; but whoever wishes to be great among you must be your servant, and whoever wishes to be first among you must be your slave; just as the Son of Man came not to be served but to serve, and to give his life a ransom for many." (Matthew 20:24-28, NRSV)

Empower us to live upside-down and backwards lives, O God—the kinds of lives in which we do things Jesus' way rather than our way.

Empower us to want to give for others rather than have others give for us.

Empower us to want to serve others rather than have others serve us.

Empower us to live lives that are based on the greatness of smallness, on the power of humility, on the gain of loss, and on the reward of sacrifice.

Amen.

DAY 282: HAVE MERCY

As they were leaving Jericho, a large crowd followed him. There were two blind men sitting by the roadside. When they heard that Jesus was passing by, they shouted, "Lord, have mercy on us, Son of David!" The crowd sternly ordered them to be quiet; but they shouted even more loudly, "Have mercy on us, Lord, Son of David!" (Matthew 20:29-31, NRSV)

Lord, have mercy on us.

You know how badly in need of your mercy we all are.

Give us awareness and acceptance of those places in our lives where we need your mercy.

Give us persistence and passion to keep asking for your mercy even over the objections of those who think and say that we should not be asking you for what we need.

Give us grace and insight always to be aware of the ways in which we have received and are receiving your mercy.

You know how badly in need of your mercy we all are.

Lord, have mercy on us.

Amen.

DAY 283: TOUCH

Jesus stood still and called them, saying, "What do you want me to do for you?" They said to him, "Lord, let our eyes be opened." Moved with compassion, Jesus touched their eyes. Immediately they regained their sight and followed him. (Matthew 20:32-34, NRSV)

Thank you, Lord, that you are moved with compassion to touch us in our wounded places and to make us whole.

Thank you, Lord, that we, having been touched by you, have the privilege to follow you.

Help us to respond to your compassion and to your touch with our following.

Amen.

DAY 284: TAKE AND USE

When they had approached Jerusalem and had come to Bethphage, at the Mount of Olives, then Jesus sent two disciples, saying to them, "Go into the village opposite you, and immediately you will find a donkey tied there and a colt with her; untie them and bring them to Me. If anyone says anything to you, you shall say, 'The Lord has need of them,' and immediately he will send them."
(Matthew 21:1-3, NASB)

What do we have that you need, Lord?

Here it is—take it and use it for your glory.

Amen.

DAY 285: FULFILL

This took place to fulfill what was spoken through the prophet:

*"Say to the daughter of Zion,
'Behold your King is coming to you,
Gentle, and mounted on a donkey,
Even on a colt, the foal of a beast of burden.'"*
(Matthew 21:4-5, NASB)

Thank you, God, that in the life, death, resurrection, and words of Jesus Christ we see and experience what we need to know about you and your ways.

Thank you that through Jesus you teach us of the value you place on humility, service, and sacrifice.

Grant that our lives will show that each day we are learning that lesson more and more.

Amen.

DAY 286: PRAISE

The disciples went and did just as Jesus had instructed them, and brought the donkey and the colt, and laid their coats on them; and He sat on the coats. Most of the crowd spread their coats in the road, and others were cutting branches from the trees and spreading them in the road. The crowds going ahead of Him, and those who followed, were shouting,

"Hosanna to the Son of David; Blessed is He who comes in the name of the Lord; Hosanna in the highest!"
(Matthew 21:6-9, NASB)

Today, and all days, may our recognition of, praise of, and dedication to Jesus show itself in our attitudes and our actions as well as in our words, O God.

Amen.

DAY 287: TURMOIL

When He had entered Jerusalem, all the city was stirred, saying, "Who is this?" And the crowds were saying,

"This is the prophet Jesus, from Nazareth in Galilee."
(Matthew 21:10-11, NASB)

Forgive us, O God, for the ways we stir up turmoil because of our fear, our pride, our envy, or our selfishness.

Forgive us also, O God, for the ways we trivialize, domesticate, and ignore the realities brought about by Jesus Christ that would, were we to give ourselves over to them, create turmoil in ways that would move us more toward you and your ways.

Forgive us our shakiness. And shake us up.

Amen.

DAY 288: HOUSE OF PRAYER

And Jesus entered the temple and drove out all those who were buying and selling in the temple, and overturned the tables of the money changers and the seats of those who were selling doves. And He said to them, "It is written, 'My house shall be called a house of prayer'; but you are making it a robbers' den." (Matthew 21:12-13, NASB)

We confess, O Lord, that sometimes our priorities get out of whack. We confess that sometimes we get way too caught up in the business of the church and give far too little attention to our relationships with you and with others.

As we conduct the business that is necessary in the church, help us to do so honestly and ethically and with a view toward bearing witness to the ways of Jesus.

Mainly, though, help us to give the vast majority of our attention to prayer—to the developing of our relationship with you—so that we will in all aspects of our church life be who we are supposed to be and act as we are supposed to act.

Amen.

DAY 289: HEALING

And the blind and the lame came to Him in the temple, and He healed them. (Matthew 21:14, NASB)

The church is the body of Christ; the church is the temple of the Lord.

And so people come to us in their needs and with their hurts.

Show us, O God, how we can offer healing to them by your grace, by your love, by your Spirit, and by your power.

Amen.

DAY 290: MOUTHS OF INFANTS

But when the chief priests and the scribes saw the wonderful things that He had done, and the children who were shouting in the temple, "Hosanna to the Son of David," they became indignant and said to Him, "Do You hear what these children are saying?" And Jesus said to them, "Yes; have you never read, 'Out of the mouth of infants and nursing babies You have prepared praise for Yourself'?" (Matthew 21:15-16, NASB)

We thank you, O God, for the privilege of maturity, for the gift of knowledge, and for the blessing of experience.

At the same time, O God, we ask you to keep us from losing or disparaging the insights of simple, childlike trust in you.

Please guard us from letting our maturity, knowledge, and experience degenerate into cynicism. Cause them instead to lead us to see the need for and value of simple faith.

Amen.

DAY 291: WITHDRAW

And He left them and went out of the city to Bethany, and spent the night there. (Matthew 21:17, NASB)

O God, sometimes the best thing we can do—the necessary thing we must do—is withdraw, rest, and get ready.

Give us the wisdom to know when such times are at hand and the discipline to make effective use of them.

Amen.

DAY 292: APPROPRIATE

Now in the morning, when He was returning to the city, He became hungry. Seeing a lone fig tree by the road, He came to it and found nothing on it except leaves only; and He said to it, "No longer shall there ever be any fruit from you." And at once the fig tree withered.

Seeing this, the disciples were amazed and asked, "How did the fig tree wither all at once?" And Jesus answered and said to them, "Truly I say to you, if you have faith and do not doubt, you will not only do what was done to the fig tree, but even if you say to this mountain, 'Be taken up and cast into the sea,' it will happen. And all things you ask in prayer, believing, you will receive." (Matthew 21:18-22, NASB)

Teach us, O Lord, to have great faith and to pray great prayers.

We don't need to move literal mountains, but it sure would help if we could get some of the metaphorical ones out of the way—or at least learn to climb or go around them.

Make our faith and our prayers not only great but appropriate—appropriate to your kingdom and appropriate to our witness.

Amen.

DAY 293: AUTHORITY

When Jesus entered the temple, the chief priests and elders of the people came to him as he was teaching. They asked, "What kind of authority do you have for doing these things? Who gave you this authority?" Jesus replied, "I have a question for you. If you tell me the answer, I'll tell you what kind of authority I have to do these things. Where did John get his authority to baptize? Did he get it from heaven or from humans?" They argued among themselves, "If we say 'from heaven,' he'll say to us, 'Then why didn't you believe him?' But we can't say 'from humans' because we're afraid of the crowd, since everyone thinks John was a prophet." Then they replied, "We don't know." Jesus also said to them, "Neither will I tell you what kind of authority I have to do these things." (Matthew 21:23-27, CEB)

Sometimes, O God, the challenging of authority is right and necessary, although we recognize that such challenges must be mounted judiciously.

Give us grace, though, not to be so arrogant as to challenge the authority of Jesus. Lead us rather to submit to his authority over our lives.

In our submission, though, lead us to do the hard and daily work of trying to ascertain his way for us, and then to live in that way with much commitment and with great joy.

Grant that our acceptance of Jesus' authority will show itself in our lifestyle as well as in our words.

Amen.

DAY 294: NOW

"What do you think? A man had two sons. Now he came to the first and said, 'Son, go and work in the vineyard today.' "'No, I don't want to,' he replied. But later he changed his mind and went. "The father said the same thing to the other son, who replied, 'Yes, sir.' But he didn't go. "Which one of these two did his father's will?" They said, "The first one." Jesus said to them, "I assure you that tax collectors and prostitutes are entering God's kingdom ahead of you. For John came to you on the righteous road, and you didn't believe him. But tax collectors and prostitutes believed him. Yet even after you saw this, you didn't change your hearts and lives and you didn't believe him." (Matthew 21:28-32, CEB)

Always remind us, O God, that the past is the past and that what is done is done.

Always remind us, O God, that right now and only right now can we love you like we should, obey like you like we should, and follow you like we should.

Always remind us, O God, that it is never too late unless we choose for it to be.

Amen.

DAY 295: GRATITUDE

"Listen to another parable. There was a landowner who planted a vineyard. He put a fence around it, dug a winepress in it, and built a tower. Then he rented it to tenant farmers and took a trip. When it was time for harvest, he sent his servants to the tenant farmers to collect his fruit. But the tenant farmers grabbed his servants. They beat some of them, and some of them they killed. Some of them they stoned to death. "Again he sent other servants, more than the first group. They treated them in the same way. Finally he sent his son to them. 'They will respect my son,' he said. "But when the tenant farmers saw the son, they said to each other, 'This is the heir. Come on, let's kill him and we'll have his inheritance.' They grabbed him, threw him out of the vineyard, and killed him. "When the owner of the vineyard comes, what will he do to those tenant farmers?" They said, "He will totally destroy those wicked farmers and rent the vineyard to other tenant farmers who will give him the fruit when it's ready." (Matthew 21:33–41, CEB)

Help us, O God, to be people who receive your good gifts with much gratitude. Help us especially to be people who receive your best gift—the gift of your Son—with much gratitude.

Grant that we will produce the kind of fruit in our lives for which you made us. Help us know the kind of fruit that you are looking for us to grow, fruit such as trust, grace, love, mercy, and peace—the kind of fruit that your Son produced and that our grateful receiving of him enables us to produce.

Amen.

DAY 296: THE LORD'S DOING

Jesus said to them, "Haven't you ever read in the scriptures, The stone that the builders rejected has become the cornerstone. The Lord has done this, and it's amazing in our eyes? Therefore, I tell you that God's kingdom will be taken away from you and will be given to a people who produce its fruit. Whoever falls on this stone will be crushed. And the stone will crush the person it falls on." (Matthew 21:42-44, CEB)

We have read the Scriptures, O Lord. We have read about who Jesus is, what Jesus did, and what Jesus reveals about your requirements of your people.

We confess that Jesus, who was rejected by many of the most religious people of his day, is the foundation and basis of your will and way for us. We confess furthermore that the fact that you revealed your will and way—indeed, yourself—in one who was despised and rejected by those who should have known better is a most amazing thing.

We confess that we are the religious people of our day, and that if we are not careful we will by our attitudes and actions reject the one who was despised and rejected.

Fill us, O God, with the knowledge that the life and way of Jesus were your doing and that, when we receive and follow him to the point that we are willing to be so different, so sacrificial, so gracious, and so loving that we might be despised and rejected, we are on our way to being who you have made and called us to be.

Amen.

DAY 297: ABOUT US

Now when the chief priests and the Pharisees heard the parable, they knew Jesus was talking about them. They were trying to arrest him, but they feared the crowds, who thought he was a prophet. (Matthew 21:45-46, CEB)

Help us realize, O Lord, when and how you speak about us. Keep us open to the challenging nature of your words.

When your words challenge, convict, and even condemn us, O Lord, keep us open to them.

Cause us to accept and assimilate such words rather than to try to get around or away from them.

Amen.

DAY 298: FILLED

Once more Jesus spoke to them in parables, saying: "The kingdom of heaven may be compared to a king who gave a wedding banquet for his son. He sent his slaves to call those who had been invited to the wedding banquet, but they would not come. Again he sent other slaves, saying, 'Tell those who have been invited: Look, I have prepared my dinner, my oxen and my fat calves have been slaughtered, and everything is ready; come to the wedding banquet.' But they made light of it and went away, one to his farm, another to his business, while the rest seized his slaves, maltreated them, and killed them. The king was enraged. He sent his troops, destroyed those murderers, and burned their city. Then he said to his slaves, 'The wedding is ready, but those invited were not worthy. Go therefore into the main streets, and invite everyone you find to the wedding banquet.' Those slaves went out into the streets and gathered all whom they found, both good and bad; so the wedding hall was filled with guests." (Matthew 22:1-10, NRSV)

We praise you, O God, that when all is said and done, your banquet hall will be filled.

We acknowledge, O God, that some of us may be surprised by who fills it.

We implore you, O God, not to let us be so blind to your great grace that we ignore or despise the invitation to be part of what you, in your great grace, are doing and to be among those whom you, in your great grace, are inviting.

Amen.

DAY 299: WITHOUT

"But when the king came in to see the guests, he noticed a man there who was not wearing a wedding robe, and he said to him, 'Friend, how did you get in here without a wedding robe?' And he was speechless. Then the king said to the attendants, 'Bind him hand and foot, and throw him into the outer darkness, where there will be weeping and gnashing of teeth.' For many are called, but few are chosen." (Matthew 22:11-14, NRSV)

Open our eyes to any ignorance or insolence we may have that causes us to presume that we belong where we don't or have a status that we don't.

Open our lives to your grace that is finally all we need to belong. Amen.

DAY 300: SINCERITY

Then the Pharisees went and plotted to entrap him in what he said. So they sent their disciples to him, along with the Herodians, saying, "Teacher, we know that you are sincere, and teach the way of God in accordance with truth, and show deference to no one; for you do not regard people with partiality. Tell us, then, what you think. Is it lawful to pay taxes to the emperor, or not?" But Jesus, aware of their malice, said, "Why are you putting me to the test, you hypocrites?" (Matthew 22:15-18, NRSV)

Help us, O Lord, to grow in character so we will ask whatever we ask you and seek whatever we seek from you out of hearts filled with sincerity and out of lives filled with integrity.

Protect us from speaking as if we have more respect for you than we do or as if we practice greater submission to you than we do.

Guard us from seeking loopholes, exceptions, or other ways out of our responsibilities.

Help us, O Lord, to grow into the kind of people who ask whatever we ask you because we want to know and who seek whatever we seek from you because we truly want to do your will.

Amen.

DAY 301: ALLEGIANCE

"Show me the coin used for the tax." And they brought him a denarius. Then he said to them, "Whose head is this, and whose title?" They answered, "The emperor's." Then he said to them, "Give therefore to the emperor the things that are the emperor's, and to God the things that are God's." When they heard this, they were amazed; and they left him and went away. (Matthew 22:19-22, NRSV)

Keep us vigilant, O God, in rendering appropriate allegiance to the various loyalties and obligations in our lives.

Keep us especially vigilant in rendering utter and ultimate allegiance to you and you alone.

Amen.

DAY 302: ESSENTIALS

The same day some Sadducees came to him, saying there is no resurrection; and they asked him a question, saying, "Teacher, Moses said, 'If a man dies childless, his brother shall marry the widow, and raise up children for his brother.' Now there were seven brothers among us; the first married, and died childless, leaving the widow to his brother. The second did the same, so also the third, down to the seventh. Last of all, the woman herself died. In the resurrection, then, whose wife of the seven will she be? For all of them had married her." (Matthew 22:23-28, NRSV)

Teach us, O God, to ask important and meaningful questions about important and meaningful subjects.

Teach us, O God, not to ask tangential questions about matters that go to the heart of the meaning of our lives under you.

Teach us, O God, not to focus on the trivial and fleeting at the cost of focusing on the essential and eternal.

Teach us, O God, to ask important and meaningful questions about important and meaningful subjects.

Amen.

DAY 303: LIVING

Jesus answered them, "You are wrong, because you know neither the scriptures nor the power of God. For in the resurrection they neither marry nor are given in marriage, but are like angels in heaven. And as for the resurrection of the dead, have you not read what was said to you by God, 'I am the God of Abraham, the God of Isaac, and the God of Jacob'? He is God not of the dead, but of the living." And when the crowd heard it, they were astounded at his teaching. (Matthew 22:29-33, NRSV)

Fill us so much with your life, O God, that we are fully alive now, even as we will be fully alive for eternity.

Fill us so much with the life of the resurrected Lord, O God, that we will live the resurrected life now as surely as we will live it after our own resurrection.

We praise you, O God, that you are God of the living.

We praise you that you are our God and that we truly live in you! Amen.

DAY 304: LOVE

When the Pharisees heard that he had silenced the Sadducees, they gathered together, and one of them, a lawyer, asked him a question to test him. "Teacher, which commandment in the law is the greatest?" He said to him, "'You shall love the Lord your God with all your heart, and with all your soul, and with all your mind.' This is the greatest and first commandment. And a second is like it: 'You shall love your neighbor as yourself.' On these two commandments hang all the law and the prophets." (Matthew 22:34-40, NRSV)

O Lord, the love to which you call us and that you command us to practice is so simple and so deep, so easy and so hard, so basic and so complex.

Forgive us for when we too easily assume that we love you as we should and that we love others as we should.

Inspire us by the example of the crucified Christ and by the presence in our lives of the crucified and resurrected Christ to live out his kind of love for you and for others.

Fill us so much with the love of Christ that loving with his love is all we want to do and all we can do.

Amen.

DAY 305: VITALITY

Now while the Pharisees were gathered together, Jesus asked them this question: "What do you think of the Messiah? Whose son is he?" They said to him, "The son of David." He said to them, "How is it then that David by the Spirit calls him Lord, saying,

'The Lord said to my Lord,
"Sit at my right hand,
until I put your enemies under your feet"'?

If David thus calls him Lord, how can he be his son?" No one was able to give him an answer, nor from that day did anyone dare to ask him any more questions. (Matthew 22:41-46, NRSV)

Protect us, O God, from relying too much on our assumptions and our traditions in our thinking about you and in the development of our relationship with you.

Open us up to whatever truth about you we are able to grasp and bear.

Empower us to live with whatever incompleteness and mystery we must.

Give us a vital and growing faith; deliver us from a stagnant life.

Amen.

DAY 306: THE GREATEST

Then Jesus spoke to the crowds and his disciples, "The legal experts and the Pharisees sit on Moses' seat. Therefore, you must take care to do everything they say. But don't do what they do. For they tie together heavy packs that are impossible to carry. They put them on the shoulders of others, but are unwilling to lift a finger to move them. Everything they do, they do to be noticed by others. They make extra-wide prayer bands for their arms and long tassels for their clothes. They love to sit in places of honor at banquets and in the synagogues. They love to be greeted with honor in the markets and to be addressed as 'Rabbi.' "But you shouldn't be called Rabbi, because you have one teacher, and all of you are brothers and sisters. Don't call anybody on earth your father, because you have one Father, who is heavenly. Don't be called teacher, because Christ is your one teacher. But the one who is greatest among you will be your servant. All who lift themselves up will be brought low. But all who make themselves low will be lifted up." (Matthew 23:1-12, CEB)

O God, forgive us and lead us away from shallowness that accepts evaluation by appearances, whether it is our evaluation of someone else or someone else's evaluation of us.

Inspire us to the kind of humble service that befits followers of the One who came not to be served but to serve.

And please protect us from that most insidious kind of pride—the kind that comes from our concluding that we are, compared with most other folks, rather humble.

Amen.

DAY 307: LEADERSHIP

"How terrible it will be for you legal experts and Phari-sees! Hypocrites! You shut people out of the kingdom of heaven. You don't enter yourselves, and you won't allow those who want to enter to do so. "How terrible it will be for you, legal experts and Pharisees! Hypocrites! You travel over sea and land to make one convert. But when they've been converted, they become twice the child of hell you are." (Matthew 23:13-15, CEB)

First of all, O God, let those of us who are leaders and teachers count on nothing but your grace to bring us into your kingdom.

Second, O God, let those of us who are leaders and teachers live so close to Christ that we think, talk, and act in ways that his followers ought to think, talk, and act.

Third, O God, let those of us who are leaders and teachers lead and teach others the truth of who you are and the truth about following a grace-filled and love-filled Lord.

Finally, O God, let those of us who are leaders and teachers lead and teach others in such a way that it is you—and not us—they are following.

Amen.

DAY 308: WORDS

"How terrible it will be for you blind guides who say, 'If people swear by the temple, it's nothing. But if people swear by the gold in the temple, they are obligated to do what they swore.' You foolish and blind people! Which is greater, the gold or the temple that makes the gold holy? You say, 'If people swear by the altar, it's nothing. But if they swear by the gift on the altar, they are obligated to do what they swore.' You blind people! Which is greater,

the gift or the altar that makes the gift holy? Therefore, those who swear by the altar swear by it and by every- thing that's on it. Those who swear by the temple swear by it and by everything that's part of it. Those who swear by heaven swear by God's throne and by the one who sits on it." (Matthew 23:16-22, CEB)

Cause us to remember, O God, that everything is yours and that you are the source of everything.

Cause us to remember, O God, that everything we say is a commitment to you.

Cause us to guard our words, O God; cause us to be people of integrity whose "Yes" is "Yes" and whose "No" is "No" and whose word is our bond to you and to others.

Amen.

DAY 309: WEIGHTY

"How terrible it will be for you legal experts and Phar- isees! Hypocrites! You give to God a tenth of mint, dill, and cumin, but you forget about the more important matters of the Law: justice, peace, and faith. You ought to give a tenth but without forgetting about those more important matters. You blind guides! You filter out an ant but swallow a camel." (Matthew 23:23-24, CEB)

Forgive us, Lord, when we do good things but neglect the best things.

Forgive us, Lord, when we follow rules but neglect people.

Forgive us, Lord, when we do the best we can but fail to trust you.

Help us, Lord, to practice the weightier matters, the things that matter the most to you: justice, mercy, and faith.

Amen.

DAY 310: CLEAN

"How terrible it will be for you legal experts and Pharisees! Hypocrites! You clean the outside of the cup and plate, but inside they are full of violence and pleasure seeking. Blind Pharisee! First clean the inside of the cup so that the outside of the cup will be clean too."
(Matthew 23:25-26, CEB)

Clean us up from the inside out, O God, so that our actions will be right because they are fueled by a right heart.
    Amen.

DAY 311: WHITEWASHED TOMBS

"How terrible it will be for you legal experts and Pharisees! Hypocrites! You are like whitewashed tombs. They look beautiful on the outside. But inside they are full of dead bones and all kinds of filth. In the same way you look righteous to people. But inside you are full of pretense and rebellion." (Matthew 23:27-28, CEB)

It's not hard to look good to people, Lord.
    It's not easy to have hearts that match our sterling reputations.
    Form us a little more each day into people of integrity. Change us on the inside so that we will truly be who you have made us to be.
    Amen.

DAY 312: HERE AND NOW

"How terrible it will be for you legal experts and Pharisees! Hypocrites! You build tombs for the prophets and

decorate the graves of the righteous. You say, 'If we had lived in our ancestors' days, we wouldn't have joined them in killing the prophets.' You testify against yourselves that you are children of those who murdered the prophets. Go ahead, complete what your ancestors did. You snakes! You children of snakes! How will you be able to escape the judgment of hell? Therefore, look, I'm sending you prophets, wise people, and legal experts. Some of them you will kill and crucify. And some you will beat in your synagogues and chase from city to city. Therefore, upon you will come all the righteous blood that has been poured out on the earth, from the blood of that righteous man Abel to the blood of Zechariah the son of Barachiah, whom you killed between the temple and the altar. I assure you that all these things will come upon this generation. " (Matthew 23:29-36, CEB)

Guard us, O God, against overconfident assertions about how we would have been and what we would have done in a time and place other than ours.

Keep us focused instead on our character and on our actions in the time and place in which we do live.

Today's trouble, after all, is sufficient for today.

Amen.

DAY 313: WILLINGNESS

"Jerusalem, Jerusalem! You who kill the prophets and stone those who were sent to you. How often I wanted to gather your people together, just as a hen gathers her chicks under her wings. But you didn't want that. Look, your house is left to you deserted. I tell you, you won't see me until you say, 'Blessings on the one who comes in the Lord's name.'" (Matthew 23:37-39, CEB)

Lord Jesus, how can we not be drawn to you by your indescribably great love and compassion?

We so often would rather go our own way than live in your grace. Forgive us. Help us. Don't give up on us.

We know that you want to gather us, to hold us, and to protect us. Help us to let you.

Amen.

DAY 314: TEMPORARY AND PERMANENT

Jesus came out from the temple and was going away when His disciples came up to point out the temple buildings to Him. And He said to them, "Do you not see all these things? Truly I say to you, not one stone here will be left upon another, which will not be torn down." (Matthew 24:1-2, NASB)

We know that things change, O God, but knowing it and accepting it are two different things.

Help us accept it.

Help us not put too much trust in things that appear permanent but are not.

Help us rather to put our trust in you whose faithfulness endures through all generations and whose purpose will be fulfilled for all eternity.

Amen.

DAY 315: BEWARE

As He was sitting on the Mount of Olives, the disciples came to Him privately, saying, "Tell us, when will these things happen, and what will be the sign of Your coming,

*and of the end of the age?" And Jesus answered and said
to them, "See to it that no one misleads you. For many
will come in My name, saying, 'I am the Christ,' and will
mislead many. You will be hearing of wars and rumors
of wars. See that you are not frightened, for those things
must take place, but that is not yet the end. For nation
will rise against nation, and kingdom against kingdom,
and in various places there will be famines and earth-
quakes. But all these things are merely the beginning of
birth pangs.* (Matthew 24:3-8, NASB)

We confess, O God, that Jesus the Christ will one day come again to
usher in your new age and to fulfill your purposes.

We affirm, O God, that along the way bad and even terrible things
have happened, do happen, and will happen.

As we navigate the events of life while looking toward the fulfillment of all things, give us insight without haughtiness, trust without
complacency, and seriousness without fear.

Give us the wisdom to follow Jesus who, after all, is the Messiah.
Help us also to pay heed only to teachers and leaders who display appropriate humility and guardedness when it comes to their own role in
your kingdom and who bear witness in their spirit to having the Spirit
of Christ.

Amen.

DAY 316: WARM

*"Then they will deliver you to tribulation, and will kill
you, and you will be hated by all nations because of My
name. At that time many will fall away and will betray
one another and hate one another. Many false prophets
will arise and will mislead many. Because lawlessness
is increased, most people's love will grow cold. But the
one who endures to the end, he will be saved. This gospel*

of the kingdom shall be preached in the whole world as a testimony to all the nations, and then the end will come." (Matthew 24:9-14, NASB)

First, Lord, strengthen and help those followers of yours who live in places where persecution is real and danger is all around. Help them to endure, and cause us to intercede for them.

Second, Lord, inspire those of us who live in places where persecution is absent and danger is for the most part imagined to be open to your love and disciplined in the ways that we stay open to it and practice it. Make your love for us and our love for each other so warm that nothing that can make it grow cold.

Amen.

DAY 317: STRAWS

"So when you see the desolating sacrilege standing in the holy place, as was spoken of by the prophet Daniel (let the reader understand), then those in Judea must flee to the mountains; the one on the housetop must not go down to take what is in the house; the one in the field must not turn back to get a coat. Woe to those who are pregnant and to those who are nursing infants in those days! Pray that your flight may not be in winter or on a sabbath. For at that time there will be great suffering, such as has not been from the beginning of the world until now, no, and never will be. And if those days had not been cut short, no one would be saved; but for the sake of the elect those days will be cut short. Then if anyone says to you, 'Look! Here is the Messiah!' or 'There he is!' —do not believe it. For false messiahs and false prophets will appear and produce great signs and omens, to lead astray, if possible, even the elect. Take note, I have told you beforehand. So, if they say to you, 'Look! He is in the

wilderness,' do not go out. If they say, 'Look! He is in the inner rooms,' do not believe it. For as the lightning comes from the east and flashes as far as the west, so will be the coming of the Son of Man. Wherever the corpse is, there the vultures will gather." (Matthew 24:15-28, NRSV)

When times get tough, O God, do not let us out of desperation grasp at straws, no matter how compelling or attractive those straws happen to look or sound.

Cause us instead to maintain a quiet, steady, vibrant trust in you, in your purposes, and in your timing.

Amen.

DAY 318: GATHERED HOME

"Immediately after the suffering of those days the sun will be darkened, and the moon will not give its light; the stars will fall from heaven, and the powers of heaven will be shaken. Then the sign of the Son of Man will appear in heaven, and then all the tribes of the earth will mourn, and they will see 'the Son of Man coming on the clouds of heaven' with power and great glory. And he will send out his angels with a loud trumpet call, and they will gather his elect from the four winds, from one end of heaven to the other." (Matthew 24:29-31, NRSV)

Inspire us, O God, to look forward to that time when we will be gathered home.

Remind us, O God, that here and now you make your home with us, so, in a real sense, we are already gathered home.

Help us, O God, to move toward being one people in these days even as we will be one people when the Great Day comes.

Amen.

DAY 319: NEAR

"From the fig tree learn its lesson: as soon as its branch becomes tender and puts forth its leaves, you know that summer is near. So also, when you see all these things, you know that he is near, at the very gates. Truly I tell you, this generation will not pass away until all these things have taken place. Heaven and earth will pass away, but my words will not pass away." (Matthew 24:32-35, NRSV)

Help us live, O Lord, in light of the fact that you are near to us—that you are present with us—all the time.

Help us live, O Lord, in light of the fact that you are near to us—right on the verge of coming back—at any time.

Amen.

DAY 320: AWAKE

"But about that day and hour no one knows, neither the angels of heaven, nor the Son, but only the Father. For as the days of Noah were, so will be the coming of the Son of Man. For as in those days before the flood they were eating and drinking, marrying and giving in marriage, until the day Noah entered the ark, and they knew nothing until the flood came and swept them all away, so too will be the coming of the Son of Man. Then two will be in the field; one will be taken and one will be left. Two women will be grinding meal together; one will be taken and one will be left. Keep awake therefore, for you do not know on what day your Lord is coming. But understand this: if the owner of the house had known in what part of the night the thief was coming, he would have stayed awake and would not have let his house be broken into.

Therefore you also must be ready, for the Son of Man is coming at an unexpected hour." (Matthew 24:36-44, NRSV)

We affirm the twin truths, O Lord, that (1) you are coming and (2) we don't know when or how you are coming.

Motivate us, therefore, to keep awake.

Help us pay close attention to our lives, rather than being lulled to sleep by their routineness.

Help us take advantage of the wait for your coming by doing your will and sharing your love, rather than being lulled to sleep by the passage of time.

Whenever you come to us and however you come to us, O Lord, help us be found ready and awake. Help us be found actively pursuing a life of love, grace, mercy, and service.

Amen.

DAY 321: FAITHFUL AND WISE

"Who then is the faithful and wise slave, whom his master has put in charge of his household, to give the other slaves their allowance of food at the proper time? Blessed is that slave whom his master will find at work when he arrives. Truly I tell you, he will put that one in charge of all his possessions. But if that wicked slave says to himself, 'My master is delayed,' and he begins to beat his fellow slaves, and eats and drinks with drunkards, the master of that slave will come on a day when he does not expect him and at an hour that he does not know. He will cut him in pieces and put him with the hypocrites, where there will be weeping and gnashing of teeth." (Matthew 24:45-51, NRSV)

During these days between your first and second Advents, O Lord, help
us be faithful and wise servants

who take our responsibilities seriously,
who enjoy our lives fully,
who treat others ethically, and
who watch for you expectantly.
Amen.

DAY 322: RECEIVE

*"Then the kingdom of heaven will be like this. Ten
bridesmaids took their lamps and went to meet the
bridegroom. Five of them were foolish, and five were wise.
When the foolish took their lamps, they took no oil with
them; but the wise took flasks of oil with their lamps. As
the bridegroom was delayed, all of them became drowsy
and slept. But at midnight there was a shout, 'Look!
Here is the bridegroom! Come out to meet him.' Then all
those bridesmaids got up and trimmed their lamps. The
foolish said to the wise, 'Give us some of your oil, for our
lamps are going out.' But the wise replied, 'No! there will
not be enough for you and for us; you had better go to
the dealers and buy some for yourselves.' And while they
went to buy it, the bridegroom came, and those who were
ready went with him into the wedding banquet; and the
door was shut. Later the other bridesmaids came also,
saying, 'Lord, lord, open to us.' But he replied, 'Truly I
tell you, I do not know you.' Keep awake therefore, for
you know neither the day nor the hour."* (Matthew
25:1-13, NRSV)

When you come, Lord, we want to be ready. We want to be in a position
to receive you and to go with you.

Help us, then, to receive you in every moment, in every thought, in every word, in every action, and in every person. Help us, then, to go with you in love, in grace, in mercy, in forgiveness, and in service.

Help us, in other words, to receive you and to go with you all the time so that when you come at the end, we'll be ready to go with you one more time.

Amen.

DAY 323: OUR BEST

"For it is as if a man, going on a journey, summoned his slaves and entrusted his property to them; to one he gave five talents, to another two, to another one, to each according to his ability. Then he went away. The one who had received the five talents went off at once and traded with them, and made five more talents. In the same way, the one who had the two talents made two more talents. But the one who had received the one talent went off and dug a hole in the ground and hid his master's money. After a long time the master of those slaves came and settled accounts with them." (Matthew 25:14-19, NRSV)

Remind us, O Lord, that we have the privilege and the responsibility to use and develop the gifts, abilities, and potentialities with which you have blessed us.

Remind us that we will not do so perfectly, thereby sparing us unnecessary frustration.

Remind us also, though, that we will be able to welcome you with joy if we have, with your help, done our best.

Amen.

DAY 324: WELL DONE

"Then the one who had received the five talents came forward, bringing five more talents, saying, 'Master, you handed over to me five talents; see, I have made five more talents.' His master said to him, 'Well done, good and trustworthy slave; you have been trustworthy in a few things, I will put you in charge of many things; enter into the joy of your master.' And the one with the two talents also came forward, saying, 'Master, you handed over to me two talents; see, I have made two more talents.' His master said to him, 'Well done, good and trustworthy slave; you have been trustworthy in a few things, I will put you in charge of many things; enter into the joy of your master.'" (Matthew 25:20-23, NRSV)

O God, help us to use well those gifts, abilities, and resources with which you bless us. Help us to use them to share your grace, love, and mercy with those we encounter.

Help us also to accept with gratitude the always increasing responsibility that becomes ours as we grow in you and in your grace.

Teach us that "Well done" implies "Now do more" rather than "Now take it easy."

Amen.

DAY 325: UNUSED

"Then the one who had received the one talent also came forward, saying, 'Master, I knew that you were a harsh man, reaping where you did not sow, and gathering where you did not scatter seed; so I was afraid, and I went and hid your talent in the ground. Here you have what is yours.' But his master replied, 'You wicked and lazy slave! You knew, did you, that I reap where I did

not sow, and gather where I did not scatter? Then you ought to have invested my money with the bankers, and on my return I would have received what was my own with interest. So take the talent from him, and give it to the one with the ten talents. For to all those who have, more will be given, and they will have an abundance; but from those who have nothing, even what they have will be taken away. As for this worthless slave, throw him into the outer darkness, where there will be weeping and gnashing of teeth.'" (Matthew 25:24-30, NRSV)

Cause us, O God, to be willing to take risks and to be daring in our use of the gifts that you have given us rather than to hoard them and to play it safe.

Remind us, O God, that you do not want those gifts back unused and unrisked but rather want us to use them to spread the love and grace of your kingdom.

Amen.

DAY 326: PRIORITIES

"When the Son of Man comes in his glory, and all the angels with him, then he will sit on the throne of his glory. All the nations will be gathered before him, and he will separate people one from another as a shepherd separates the sheep from the goats, and he will put the sheep at his right hand and the goats at the left. Then the king will say to those at his right hand, 'Come, you that are blessed by my Father, inherit the kingdom prepared for you from the foundation of the world; for I was hungry and you gave me food, I was thirsty and you gave me something to drink, I was a stranger and you welcomed me, I was naked and you gave me clothing,

I was sick and you took care of me, I was in prison and
you visited me.'" (Matthew 25:31-36, NRSV)

We praise you, O God, that the kingdom is prepared for those who feed
the hungry, who give drink to the thirsty, who welcome the strangers,
who clothe the naked, who take care of the sick, and who visit the
prisoners.

We praise you for it, even as we ponder what we spent our time,
energy, and other resources on yesterday and what we spend our time,
energy, and other resources doing every day.

Lord, have mercy.

Lord, give us the right priorities.

Amen.

DAY 327: WHEN?

"Then the righteous will answer him, 'Lord, when was
it that we saw you hungry and gave you food, or thirsty
and gave you something to drink? And when was it that
we saw you a stranger and welcomed you, or naked and
gave you clothing? And when was it that we saw you sick
or in prison and visited you?' And the king will answer
them, 'Truly I tell you, just as you did it to one of the least
of these who are members of my family, you did it to me.'
Then he will say to those at his left hand, 'You that are
accursed, depart from me into the eternal fire prepared
for the devil and his angels; for I was hungry and you
gave me no food, I was thirsty and you gave me nothing
to drink, I was a stranger and you did not welcome
me, naked and you did not give me clothing, sick and
in prison and you did not visit me.' Then they also will
answer, 'Lord, when was it that we saw you hungry or
thirsty or a stranger or naked or sick or in prison, and
did not take care of you?' Then he will answer them,

'Truly I tell you, just as you did not do it to one of the least of these, you did not do it to me.' And these will go away into eternal punishment, but the righteous into eternal life." (Matthew 25:37-46, NRSV)

Lord, give us eyes to see the hurting people who are all around us. Give us hearts that care enough to try to help heal their hurts.

Guard us from the kind of calculating self-interest that connects our concern and help with our possible reward.

Help us see you in those who are oppressed, poor, sick, incarcerated, hungry, thirsty, lonely, and outcast, but not at the cost of failing to see them for who they are.

Grant that our care, concern, and help will come to be as natural to us as our lack of care, concern, and help tends to be.

Amen.

DAY 328: CONSPIRACY

When Jesus had finished all these words, He said to His disciples, "You know that after two days the Passover is coming, and the Son of Man is to be handed over for crucifixion." Then the chief priests and the elders of the people were gathered together in the court of the high priest, named Caiaphas; and they plotted together to seize Jesus by stealth and kill Him. But they were saying, "Not during the festival, otherwise a riot might occur among the people." (Matthew 26:1-5, NASB)

Are we conspiratorial by nature? Or by training? Or by both? Regardless, we acknowledge and confess that we do like to plot and plan.

Lead us, O God, so our plotting and planning will be toward a positive end and not a negative one, toward a constructive end and not a destructive one.

Lead us so that our plotting and planning will carry us to a greater acceptance of and following of Jesus and not to the neglect or rejection of Jesus' claims on our lives.

Grant, O God, that our conspiracies will be conspiracies of love, grace, forgiveness, and kindness rather than conspiracies of hate, revenge, cruelty, and apathy.

Amen.

DAY 329: REMEMBERED

Now when Jesus was in Bethany, at the home of Simon the leper, a woman came to Him with an alabaster vial of very costly perfume, and she poured it on His head as He reclined at the table. But the disciples were indignant when they saw this, and said, "Why this waste? For this perfume might have been sold for a high price and the money given to the poor." But Jesus, aware of this, said to them, "Why do you bother the woman? For she has done a good deed to Me. For you always have the poor with you; but you do not always have Me. For when she poured this perfume on My body, she did it to prepare Me for burial. Truly I say to you, wherever this gospel is preached in the whole world, what this woman has done will also be spoken of in memory of her." (Matthew 26:6-13, NASB)

If we are going to be remembered at all, O Lord, let us be remembered for the ways we gave ourselves away out of love for you and in service to you.

Given that you taught us to see you in other people—especially those who have the greatest need—if we are going to be remembered at all, let us be remembered for the ways we gave ourselves away for the sake of and in service to other people.

Amen.

DAY 330: BETRAYAL

Then one of the twelve, named Judas Iscariot, went to the chief priests and said, "What are you willing to give me to betray Him to you?" And they weighed out thirty pieces of silver to him. From then on he began looking for a good opportunity to betray Jesus. (Matthew 26:14-16, NASB)

It is unlikely that we will look for an opportunity to betray you, Lord.

It is much more likely that our betrayals will be of the careless and thoughtless variety.

Train us in tending to our relationship with you so that we will by our thoughts, motives, words, and actions display faithfulness to you.

Amen.

DAY 331: SMALL THINGS

Now on the first day of Unleavened Bread the disciples came to Jesus and asked, "Where do You want us to prepare for You to eat the Passover?" And He said, "Go into the city to a certain man, and say to him, 'The Teacher says, "My time is near; I am to keep the Passover at your house with My disciples."'" The disciples did as Jesus had directed them; and they prepared the Passover. (Matthew 26:17-19, NASB)

Make us faithful in the small things, O Lord, that we might learn how to be faithful in the big things.

Remind us that we never know what big things the small things might lead to.

Amen.

DAY 332: LORD

*When it was evening, he took his place with the twelve;
and while they were eating, he said, "Truly I tell you,
one of you will betray me." And they became greatly
distressed and began to say to him one after another,
"Surely not I, Lord?" He answered, "The one who has
dipped his hand into the bowl with me will betray me.
The Son of Man goes as it is written of him, but woe to
that one by whom the Son of Man is betrayed! It would
have been better for that one not to have been born."
Judas, who betrayed him, said, "Surely not I, Rabbi?"
He replied, "You have said so." (Matthew 26:20-25,
NRSV)*

Lord Jesus,

It's an admittedly fine but nonetheless important distinction: when
you said that one of the Twelve would betray you, Judas asked, "Surely
not I, Teacher?" while the rest asked, "Surely not I, Lord?"

Judas betrayed you.

The rest denied you by words or by actions or by both.

So even if we acknowledge and serve you as Lord, we will still fail
and fall.

Grant, though, O Lord, that we will have the kind of submitted
and obedient relationship with you that will lead us always to try to stay
close to you and always to try to be true to you.

You are a great Teacher and we learn from you.

Be our Lord that we might live in you.

Amen.

DAY 333: PARTICIPATION & ANTICIPATION

While they were eating, Jesus took a loaf of bread, and after blessing it he broke it, gave it to the disciples, and said, "Take, eat; this is my body." Then he took a cup, and after giving thanks he gave it to them, saying, "Drink from it, all of you; for this is my blood of the covenant, which is poured out for many for the forgiveness of sins. I tell you, I will never again drink of this fruit of the vine until that day when I drink it new with you in my Father's kingdom." When they had sung the hymn, they went out to the Mount of Olives. (Matthew 26:26-30, NRSV)

Thank you, Lord, that when we eat the bread and drink the cup of the Eucharist, we are both remembering what you have done and anticipating what you will do.

Thank you, Lord, that in eating the bread and drinking the cup, we both participate in the fellowship we have with you and our other brothers and sisters here and now and anticipate the fellowship we will have with you and our other brothers and sisters there and then.

Amen.

DAY 334: AHEAD

Then Jesus said to them, "You will all become deserters because of me this night; for it is written, 'I will strike the shepherd, and the sheep of the flock will be scattered.' But after I am raised up, I will go ahead of you to Galilee." Peter said to him, "Though all become deserters because of you, I will never desert you." Jesus said to him, "Truly I tell you, this very night, before the cock crows, you will deny me three times." Peter said to him, "Even though I

*must die with you, I will not deny you." And so said all
the disciples.* (Matthew 26:31-35, NRSV)

We praise you, O Lord, that even though you know we will fail, you
nonetheless plan to meet us on the other side of our failure.

We praise you, O Lord, that even when we do fail, you nonetheless
meet us on the other side of our failure.

Still—help us grow in our commitment and willingness to give up
our lives so we will, in our lives and by our lives, become less and less
likely to fail you and more and more likely to bear bold and honest
witness to our relationship with you through our risk-taking and self-
denying actions.

Amen.

DAY 335: INSIGHT & COURAGE

*Then Jesus went with them to a place called Gethse-
mane; and he said to his disciples, "Sit here while I
go over there and pray." He took with him Peter and
the two sons of Zebedee, and began to be grieved and
agitated. Then he said to them, "I am deeply grieved,
even to death; remain here, and stay awake with me."*
(Matthew 26:36-38, NRSV)

Give us insight and courage, O Lord, to understand and to live in light
of the fact that we of the church are the Body of Christ in this world.

Give us insight and courage, O Lord, to understand and to live
in light of the fact that the incarnation, the presence of Christ in this
world, continues through us.

Give us insight and courage, O Lord, to understand and to live in
light of the fact that we are to be deeply grieved, even to death, over the
plight of the people around us.

Give us insight and courage, O Lord, to understand and to live in
light of the fact that we are to give ourselves up in obedience to God and
for the sake of the people around us.

Give us insight and courage, O Lord, to understand and to live in light of the fact that to stay awake with you in these days is to be your sacrificial presence in these days.

Amen.

DAY 336: WHAT YOU WANT

And going a little farther, he threw himself on the ground and prayed, "My Father, if it is possible, let this cup pass from me; yet not what I want but what you want." (Matthew 26:39, NRSV)

We praise you, O God, for the full humanity of Jesus your Son that we see both in his plea to be allowed to avoid his suffering if possible and in his commitment to embrace his suffering if he must.

Cause his life to be so present in ours that we exhibit the same kind of full humanity. May we be honest about our fears concerning the sacrificial life to which you call us, even as we are firm in our dedication to live it out no matter what the cost.

"Not what we want but what you want"—this is our prayer, God help us.

Amen.

DAY 337: A WILLING SPIRIT

Then he came to the disciples and found them sleeping; and he said to Peter, "So, could you not stay awake with me one hour? Stay awake and pray that you may not come into the time of trial; the spirit indeed is willing, but the flesh is weak." (Matthew 26:40-41, NRSV)

We acknowledge, O Lord, that in this life our spirits cannot be separated from our bodies. We cannot experience spiritual things unless we experience them in and through our bodies.

We also acknowledge, though, that sometimes what your Spirit leads us to do we don't do, even if we want to do it, and sometimes what your Spirit leads us not to do we do, even if we don't want to do it.

We must acknowledge also, however, that sometimes even our spirit is not willing.

Give us through your Spirit, O Lord, the mind of Christ, so that in the totality of our being we both want to do your will and try to do your will.

Amen.

DAY 338: GOING

Again he went away for the second time and prayed, "My Father, if this cannot pass unless I drink it, your will be done." Again he came and found them sleeping, for their eyes were heavy. So leaving them again, he went away and prayed for the third time, saying the same words. Then he came to the disciples and said to them, "Are you still sleeping and taking your rest? See, the hour is at hand, and the Son of Man is betrayed into the hands of sinners. Get up, let us be going. See, my betrayer is at hand." (Matthew 26:42-46, NRSV)

Let us be going, O Lord.

Let us be going, O Lord, to face what we must face as your followers.

Let us be going, O Lord, to drink the cup that we must drink as your followers.

Let us be going, O Lord, to face the opposition we must face as your followers.

Let us be going, O Lord, to live in your difficult and wonderful will as your followers.

Let us be going, O Lord, to grow into the kind of following that we should practice as your followers.

Let us be going, O Lord.

Amen.

DAY 339: INTIMACY

While he was still speaking, Judas, one of the twelve, arrived; with him was a large crowd with swords and clubs, from the chief priests and the elders of the people. Now the betrayer had given them a sign, saying, "The one I will kiss is the man; arrest him." At once he came up to Jesus and said, "Greetings, Rabbi!" and kissed him. Jesus said to him, "Friend, do what you are here to do." Then they came and laid hands on Jesus and arrested him. (Matthew 26:47-50, NRSV)

We thank you, O God, that we have the opportunity for an intimately personal relationship with Jesus Christ. Help us develop that relationship in appropriate ways. Help us be obedient, faithful, and open.

Protect us from trying to use that relationship in inappropriate ways. Guard us against attempted manipulation, sought advantage, and selfish motives.

Remind us, O God, that a kiss is not just a kiss, but that a kiss can reveal any number of motivations and desires. May our expressions of affection to you be legitimate, honest, and appropriate.

Amen.

DAY 340: SHEATHED

Suddenly, one of those with Jesus put his hand on his sword, drew it, and struck the slave of the high priest, cutting off his ear. Then Jesus said to him, "Put your sword back into its place; for all who take the sword will perish by the sword. Do you think that I cannot appeal to my Father, and he will at once send me more than twelve legions of angels? But how then would the scriptures be fulfilled, which say it must happen in this way?" At that hour Jesus said to the crowds, "Have you come out with

*swords and clubs to arrest me as though I were a bandit?
Day after day I sat in the temple teaching, and you did
not arrest me. But all this has taken place, so that the
scriptures of the prophets may be fulfilled." Then all the
disciples deserted him and fled.* (Matthew 26:51-56,
NRSV)

We thank you, O God, that you sent your Son Jesus into this war-torn
and conflict-riddled world to be the Prince of Peace.

We thank you that the angel who announced his birth to the shep-
herds spoke of "peace among those whom [God] favors" (Luke 2:14).

We thank you that he, until the very end, responded to fear with
faith, to anger with grace, to hate with love, and to conflict with peace.

We thank you that he, although he had a more powerful sword
available to him than we could even begin to imagine, kept it sheathed.

Help us, O God, as followers of the Prince of Peace, to keep our
pitiful swords put away, too, and instead to use his arsenal of faith,
grace, love, and peace.

Amen.

DAY 341: ENDURANCE

*Those who had arrested Jesus took him to Caiaphas the
high priest, in whose house the scribes and the elders had
gathered. But Peter was following him at a distance, as
far as the courtyard of the high priest; and going inside,
he sat with the guards in order to see how this would
end.* (Matthew 26:57-58, NRSV)

Sometimes, O Lord, we follow you and follow you and follow you, only
to decide at some crucial point to sit down and watch to see how it will
all turn out.

Give us the desire and the courage to follow and to endure until the
end, and beyond.

Amen.

DAY 342: TESTIMONY

Now the chief priests and the whole council were looking for false testimony against Jesus so that they might put him to death, but they found none, though many false witnesses came forward. At last two came forward and said, "This fellow said, 'I am able to destroy the temple of God and to build it in three days.'" The high priest stood up and said, "Have you no answer? What is it that they testify against you?" But Jesus was silent. (Matthew 26:59-63a)

Work on our hearts, O Lord, so we will look for the truth about you so we can believe, rather than look for the false about you so that we cannot believe.

Protect us from listening to those who hear and repeat your words only in terms of wooden literalism, and free us instead to listen to those who have ears to hear, spirits to receive, and mouths to speak the truth of your words.

Help us, O Lord—for you have spoken and we must choose whether and how we will hear.

Amen.

DAY 343: WITNESS

Then the high priest said to him, "I put you under oath before the living God, tell us if you are the Messiah, the Son of God." Jesus said to him, "You have said so. But I tell you,

From now on you will see the Son of Man seated at the right hand of Power and coming on the clouds of heaven."

Then the high priest tore his clothes and said, "He has blasphemed! Why do we still need witnesses? You have now heard his blasphemy. What is your verdict?" They answered, "He deserves death." Then they spat in his face and struck him; and some slapped him, saying, "Prophesy to us, you Messiah! Who is it that struck you?" (Matthew 26:63b-68, NRSV)

We praise you, O Lord, that you accepted the suffering and death that you did not deserve because you are the Messiah, the Son of God, and the Son of Man, and because you are the One who came to be God with us, to be the kingdom of God among us, and to be the Suffering Servant.

We thank you that you showed us that the way to glory is the way of service, sacrifice, and love.

We ask for the grace to live as your followers in ways that bear witness to the Messiah that you are and not to the one that we might want you to be.

Amen.

DAY 344: WEEPING

Now Peter was sitting outside in the courtyard. A servant-girl came to him and said, "You also were with Jesus the Galilean." But he denied it before all of them, saying, "I do not know what you are talking about." When he went out to the porch, another servant-girl saw him, and she said to the bystanders, "This man was with Jesus of Nazareth." Again he denied it with an oath, "I do not know the man." After a little while the bystanders came up and said to Peter, "Certainly you are also one of them, for your accent betrays you." Then he began to curse, and he swore an oath, "I do not know the man!" At that moment the cock crowed. Then

Peter remembered what Jesus had said: "Before the cock crows, you will deny me three times." And he went out and wept bitterly. (Matthew 26:69-75, NRSV)

How long, O Lord, will we do what we do not want to do?

How long, O Lord, will we not do what we want to do?

How long, O Lord, will we weep bitterly over our failures that are motivated by our misguided drive for self-preservation?

How long, O Lord, will we fail to align ourselves with you in grace-filled obedience and self-emptying sacrifice?

Sometimes our hearts break over the kinds of heart that our actions show we still have. Sometimes we are shocked at how far we still have to go. Help us, O Lord, to face up to where we are and to trust your grace to lead us to where we need to be.

Amen.

DAY 345: HANDING OVER

Now when morning came, all the chief priests and the elders of the people conferred together against Jesus to put Him to death; and they bound Him, and led Him away and delivered Him to Pilate the governor. (Matthew 27:1-2, NASB)

This morning—or this afternoon—or this evening—here you are again and here we are again and here it all is again, and so we decide yet again what to do with you, O Lord.

We cannot hand you over or pass you along or wash our hands of you—we must deal with you.

Cause us to see your presence as the miracle of grace that it is. Cause us to see you as the gift of love that you are.

Yes, your presence can cause us pain—the kind of pain that comes from seeing ourselves in your bright and revealing light.

But it is worth it, O Lord—it is worth it.

Still, we want to hand you over to others so they can know you and your simultaneously affirming and challenging love.

But as we hand you over, may we keep one hand on you.

Amen.

DAY 346: BLOOD MONEY

Then when Judas, who had betrayed Him, saw that He had been condemned, he felt remorse and returned the thirty pieces of silver to the chief priests and elders, saying, "I have sinned by betraying innocent blood." But they said, "What is that to us? See to that yourself!" And he threw the pieces of silver into the temple sanctuary and departed; and he went away and hanged himself. The chief priests took the pieces of silver and said, "It is not lawful to put them into the temple treasury, since it is the price of blood." And they conferred together and with the money bought the Potter's Field as a burial place for strangers. For this reason that field has been called the Field of Blood to this day. Then that which was spoken through Jeremiah the prophet was fulfilled: "And they took the thirty pieces of silver, the price of the one whose price had been set by the sons of Israel; and they gave them for the Potter's Field, as the Lord directed me." (Matthew 27:3-10, NASB)

We would never betray you, so we tell ourselves, O Lord—and we certainly would not betray you for money.

And yet—

You said that insofar as we tend to or neglect the needs of those who are hungry, sick, naked, or in prison, we tend to or neglect you. It is not a stretch, therefore, to say that insofar as we are faithful to them, we are faithful to you, and insofar as we betray them, we betray you.

You also said that where our treasure is, there our heart will be too.

And so—

Give us the willingness to face up to how we are betraying you by betraying others—in particular, others who are desperately hurting—through the ways we use our money or the ways we save our money or the ways we invest our money.

Give us the insight, the compassion, and the courage to investigate how people—even and maybe especially people on the other side of the world and definitely at the other end of the economic ladder—are negatively affected by the ways that we more affluent Christians spend, save, and invest our money.

Do we hold blood money in our pockets or in our products?

Forgive us, O Lord, for our betrayals of you.

Help us, O Lord, to spend the rest of our lives working at making amends.

Amen.

DAY 347: SILENCE

Jesus was brought before the governor. The governor said, "Are you the king of the Jews?" Jesus replied, "That's what you say." But he didn't answer when the chief priests and elders accused him. Then Pilate said, "Don't you hear the testimony they bring against you?" But he didn't answer, not even a single word. So the governor was greatly amazed. (Matthew 27:11-14, CEB)

Teach us, O God, that sometimes, no matter what we say, our words will make no difference. Remind us, O God, that sometimes people's minds are so made up or so closed that even our truest words will not matter. In those times, help us see that the greatest truth will be expressed through silence.

Teach us, O God, of the wisdom of silence. Show us, O God, when it is best not to say a thing, even to defend ourselves.

Amen.

DAY 348: CHOICE

It was customary during the festival for the governor to release to the crowd one prisoner, whomever they might choose. At that time there was a well-known prisoner named Jesus Barabbas. When the crowd had come together, Pilate asked them, "Whom would you like me to release to you, Jesus Barabbas or Jesus who is called Christ?" He knew that the leaders of the people had handed him over because of jealousy. While he was serving as judge, his wife sent this message to him, "Leave that righteous man alone. I've suffered much today in a dream because of him." But the chief priests and the elders persuaded the crowds to ask for Barabbas and kill Jesus. The governor said, "Which of the two do you want me to release to you?" "Barabbas," they replied. Pilate said, "Then what should I do with Jesus who is called Christ?" They all said, "Crucify him!" But he said, "Why? What wrong has he done?" They shouted even louder, "Crucify him!" (Matthew 27:15-23, CEB)

While we acknowledge the concern that prompted the message from Pilate's wife, we must challenge the value of her advice, O Lord, for it was not an option for her husband to have nothing to do with that innocent man, Jesus.

It is not an option for us either.

While Pilate's options were to release Jesus or to have him crucified, our options are to

(1) try to live a life that ignores him—which won't work because he's always there,

(2) try to live a life motivated by our self-interest—which won't work because down that way lies emptiness and frustration, or

(3) try to live a life based on following him—which will work but which is at the same time the easiest and the hardest way of all.

Today—again—we choose.

Give us sufficient wisdom, courage, and faith to choose well and then to live well, knowing that everything has to do with that Innocent Man.

Amen.

DAY 349: ON US

Pilate saw that he was getting nowhere and that a riot was starting. So he took water and washed his hands in front of the crowd. "I'm innocent of this man's blood," he said. "It's your problem." All the people replied, "Let his blood be on us and on our children." Then he released Barabbas to them. He had Jesus whipped, then handed him over to be crucified. (Matthew 27:24-26, CEB)

What the people meant when they said "His blood be on us and on our children" was that they were willing to accept the responsibility for the crucifixion of Jesus. What Pilate meant when he said "I am innocent of this man's blood" was that he was not willing to accept responsibility for the crucifixion of Jesus.

It is likely that the people didn't realize the gravity of what they were saying. It is possible that they were caught up in a mob mentality. It is possible that the many in the middle were swayed by the passions of the extremists.

It is likely that Pilate did realize the absurdity of what he was saying. It is possible that he was caught up in political survival mode. It is possible that he was afraid of the situation in which he found himself.

We would never say, "His blood be on us and on our children," but, dear God, we are responsible nonetheless. After all, it is for our healing that he suffered.

We would never say, "I am innocent of this man's blood"—although sometimes we try to ignore or to evade our responsibility—but, dear God, we are responsible nonetheless After all, it is for our sins that he died.

There is another sense in which his blood can be on us, O God—your Book teaches us that our sins can be covered by his blood.

"His blood be on us"—cause us to accept our responsibility, O God.

"His blood be on us"—enable us to know your forgiveness, O God. Amen.

DAY 350: MOCKERY

The governor's soldiers took Jesus into the governor's house, and they gathered the whole company of soldiers around him. They stripped him and put a red military coat on him. They twisted together a crown of thorns and put it on his head. They put a stick in his right hand. Then they bowed down in front of him and mocked him, saying, "Hey! King of the Jews!" After they spit on him, they took the stick and struck his head again and again. When they finished mocking him, they stripped him of the military coat and put his own clothes back on him. They led him away to crucify him. (Matthew 27:27-31, CEB)

The soldiers mocked Jesus by hailing him as "King of the Jews" while treating him as if he was anything but a King. Indeed, they treated him as if he were subject to whatever insults and abuse they wished to inflict on him.

Give us courage, O God, to face up to whatever ways, be they obvious or subtle, that we mock Jesus by calling him our King while at the same time behaving in ways or by giving in to motivations that dishonor him.

Give us the grace to think thoughts and to carry out actions that reflect our service to and our following of Jesus Christ our King. Give us the grace to mean what we say when we call him "King," to live lives that match our words, to say words that match our lives, and to have spirits that lead us, when it comes to Jesus, to true words and true actions.

Amen.

DAY 351: CARRY HIS CROSS

As they were going out, they found Simon, a man from Cyrene. They forced him to carry his cross. (Matthew 27:32, CEB)

Compel us, O God, to carry the cross of Jesus Christ as we live in this day.

Compel us, O God, to take up our cross and follow Jesus.

Compel us, O God, to live lives so filled with the grace and love of Jesus that we gladly give ourselves away day by day and moment by moment for the sake of that grace and love.

Amen.

DAY 352: THIS IS JESUS

When they came to a place called Golgotha, which means Skull Place, they gave Jesus wine mixed with vinegar to drink. But after tasting it, he didn't want to drink it. After they crucified him, they divided up his clothes among them by drawing lots. They sat there, guarding him. They placed above his head the charge against him. It read, "This is Jesus, the king of the Jews." (Matthew 27:33-37, CEB)

Grant, O God, that when we think about who Jesus is, we will always think of him hanging on the cross, giving his all.

Grant, O God, that when we think about what it is to be a follower of Jesus, we will always think of him hanging on the cross, giving his all. Amen.

DAY 353: COME DOWN

They crucified with him two outlaws, one on his right side and one on his left. Those who were walking by insulted Jesus, shaking their heads and saying, "So you were going to destroy the temple and rebuild it in three days, were you? Save yourself! If you are God's Son, come down from the cross." In the same way, the chief priests, along with the legal experts and the elders, were making fun of him, saying, "He saved others, but he can't save himself. He's the king of Israel, so let him come down from the cross now. Then we'll believe in him. He trusts in God, so let God deliver him now if he wants to. He said, 'I'm God's Son.'" The outlaws who were crucified with him insulted him in the same way.
(Matthew 27:38-44, CEB)

"If you are the Son of God," they said to Jesus, "come down from the cross."

Never let us forget, O God, that he did not come down from the cross precisely because he was the Son of God.

Never let us forget, O God, that we are not to give up our cross precisely because we are the children of God, too.

Continuously teach us how, in being faithful in bearing the cross, we are faithful in following Jesus. Continuously teach us how, in giving up our lives, we find them.

Amen.

DAY 354: FORSAKEN

From noon until three in the afternoon the whole earth was dark. At about three Jesus cried out with a loud shout, "Eli, Eli, lama sabachthani," which means, "My God, my God, why have you left me?" After hearing him, some standing there said, "He's calling Elijah." One of them ran over, took a sponge full of vinegar, and put it on a pole. He offered it to Jesus to drink. But the rest of them said, "Let's see if Elijah will come and save him." (Matthew 27:45-49, CEB)

It was a heart-wrenching, gut-wrenching, and spirit-wrenching prayer that Jesus voiced in the throes of death as he hung on the cross.

It was a prayer that reflected what he was experiencing.

Sometimes, O God, we in our pain cry out in a similar way. May it be an honest prayer when we pray it, and not one fueled by our tendency toward drama and hyperbole.

Sometimes, O God, our pain is so real and our sense of your absence is so real that all we can do is cry out to you.

Remind us, O God, even as we cry out to you, that joy comes in the morning and that resurrection follows crucifixion.

Amen.

DAY 355: GOD'S SON

Again Jesus cried out with a loud shout. Then he died. Look, the curtain of the sanctuary was torn in two from top to bottom. The earth shook, the rocks split, and the bodies of many holy people who had died were raised. After Jesus' resurrection they came out of their graves and went into the holy city where they appeared to many people. When the centurion and those with him who were guarding Jesus saw the earthquake and what had just happened, they were filled with awe and said, "This was certainly God's Son." (Matthew 27:50-54, CEB)

Keep us attuned, O God, to the ongoing results of and the ongoing effect of the death of your Son Jesus.

Keep us aware, O God, of how things have changed and are changing, both in your vast creation and in the lives of people, because of the death of Jesus.

Keep us amazed, O God, at what the crucifixion shows us about who Jesus was and who Jesus is.

Amen.

DAY 356: ENDURING FAITH

Many women were watching from a distance. They had followed Jesus from Galilee to serve him. Among them were Mary Magdalene, Mary the mother of James and Joseph, and the mother of Zebedee's sons. (Matthew 27:55-56, CEB)

Give us the kind of grace and faith that the women at the cross had, O God—the kind of grace and faith that endures to the end and that follows Jesus wherever he goes, no matter the risk or the cost.

Amen.

DAY 357: LEAVING AND STAYING

That evening a man named Joseph came. He was a rich man from Arimathea who had become a disciple of Jesus. He came to Pilate and asked for Jesus' body.

Pilate gave him permission to take it. Joseph took the body, wrapped it in a clean linen cloth, and laid it in his own new tomb, which he had carved out of the rock. After he rolled a large stone at the door of the tomb, he went away. Mary Magdalene and the other Mary were there, sitting in front of the tomb. (Matthew 27:57-61, CEB)

Joseph of Arimathea and the two Marys did the best they could do for Jesus after he died. Joseph used his status and his wealth to have Jesus entombed, while the two Marys used their compassion and their time to show their respect for Jesus.

Joseph went away from the tomb while the two Marys stayed there. But they all did their best.

Help us to do our best in the face of the reality of Jesus' crucifixion, O God. As it is appropriate, lead us to go on about our business and about your business. As it is appropriate, lead us to sit, to reflect, and to wait.

Whatever we do, O God, let it be done out of devotion to Jesus.

Whatever we do, O God, let us live in light of the twin facts that Jesus gave up his life and that Jesus calls us to give up our lives.

Amen.

DAY 358: SECURE

The next day, which was the day after Preparation Day, the chief priests and the Pharisees gathered before Pilate. They said, "Sir, we remember that while that deceiver was still alive he said, 'After three days I will arise.' Therefore, order the grave to be sealed until the third day. Otherwise, his disciples may come and steal the body and tell the people, 'He's been raised from the dead.' This last deception will be worse than the first."

Pilate replied, "You have soldiers for guard duty. Go and make it as secure as you know how." Then they went and secured the tomb by sealing the stone and posting the guard. (Matthew 27:62-66, CEB)

They used a stone to try to block the power of the resurrection.
They failed.

Protect us, O God, from the futility of trying to shut ourselves off from the power of the resurrection and from the true life that can be ours in the resurrected Lord.

Protect us from the attempt to secure ourselves from the risk inherent in the resurrected Jesus; lead us instead to secure ourselves in the risk inherent in the resurrected Jesus.

Lead us into the wonderfully dangerous life that is ours through the life of the resurrected Lord that is present in us.

Amen.

DAY 359: DEAD OR ALIVE

After the Sabbath, at dawn on the first day of the week, Mary Magdalene and the other Mary came to look at the tomb. Look, there was a great earthquake, for an angel from the Lord came down from heaven. Coming to the stone, he rolled it away and sat on it. Now his face was like lightning and his clothes as white as snow. The guards were so terrified of him that they shook with fear and became like dead men. (Matthew 28:1-4, CEB)

Grant, O God, that we will apprehend and experience your gracious acts of intervention in our world in ways that will make us alive, as you intend us to be, and not dead, as we tend to be.

Thank you for the real life that can be ours through the resurrection of your Son Jesus. Help us not miss it because we are not looking for it, or because when we see it we are afraid of it.

Too many people are among the walking and breathing dead, O God. Make us so alive with the life of the resurrected Jesus that they can catch it from us.

Amen.

DAY 360: REVERENCE AND JOY

But the angel said to the women, "Don't be afraid. I know that you are looking for Jesus who was crucified. He isn't here, because he's been raised from the dead, just as he said. Come, see the place where they laid him. Now hurry, go and tell his disciples, 'He's been raised from the dead. He's going on ahead of you to Galilee. You will see him there.' I've given the message to you." With great fear and excitement, they hurried away from the tomb and ran to tell his disciples. But Jesus met them and greeted them. They came and grabbed his feet and worshiped him. Then Jesus said to them, "Don't be afraid. Go and tell my brothers that I am going into Galilee. They will see me there." (Matthew 28:5-10, CEB)

On one hand, we need to focus on the crucified Jesus. He did, after all, give his life for us and he did, after all, teach us by his words and by his life that those who lose their lives will find them.

On the other hand, we need to focus on the resurrected Jesus. He is, after all, not in his grave and he is, after all, alive in and among us where we can and do experience him.

Cause us constantly to remember, O God, that Jesus died and that Jesus lives.

Fill us with the appropriate reverence, that we will worship him, and with the appropriate joy, that we will serve him.

Amen.

DAY 361: STILL TOLD

Now as the women were on their way, some of the guards came into the city and told the chief priests everything that had happened. They met with the elders and decided to give a large sum of money to the soldiers. They told them, "Say that Jesus' disciples came at night and stole his body while you were sleeping. And if the governor hears about this, we will take care of it with him so you will have nothing to worry about." So the soldiers took the money and did as they were told. And this report has spread throughout all Judea to this very day. (Matthew 28:11-15, CEB)

So fill us with the presence of the resurrected Jesus, with real life, O God, that our lives will continue the true story of his resurrection.

Protect us from the kind of dead and deadening lives, O God, that would make it hard for anyone to believe that we serve a risen Savior.

Amen.

DAY 362: WORSHIP AND DOUBT

Now the eleven disciples went to Galilee, to the mountain where Jesus told them to go. When they saw him, they worshiped him, but some doubted. (Matthew 28:16-17, CEB)

O Lord, may our experience of you be as real to us as that of those who were privileged to see you in your resurrected state.

O Lord, may our response to our experience of you be to worship you—to serve you by loving you with all our heart, soul, mind, and strength and by loving our neighbors as we love ourselves.

O Lord, may our doubts that come to us even in the midst of our experience of you and our worship of you serve in the long run to strengthen the real faith that we need in living real lives in this real world.

Amen.

DAY 363: GO THEREFORE

Jesus came near and spoke to them, "I've received all authority in heaven and on earth. Therefore, go and make disciples of all nations, baptizing them in the name of the Father and of the Son and of the Holy Spirit, teaching them to obey everything that I've commanded you." (Matthew 28:18-20a, CEB)

Give us grace, love, faith, and hope enough, O Lord, that we will live every moment of our lives sharing with others what we have received from you.

Inspire us to not keep these great gifts to ourselves, O Lord, but gladly and willingly to give them away. Such gladness and willingness will constitute perhaps the greatest evidence that we have received those gifts from you.

They will, after all, know we are Christians by our love.

Amen.

DAY 364: I AM WITH YOU

"Look, I myself will be with you every day..." (Matthew 28:20b, CEB)

Thank you, Lord Jesus, that you always have been, always are, and always will be with us.

Amen.

DAY 365: THE END

". . . until the end of this present age." (Matthew 28:20b, CEB)

O God, the end will come when it comes. When it comes, all will be as it should be. Until then, all is not as it should be. In the meantime, help us grow toward being all we can be in Christ. Help us do all we can to always be contributing to making things better.

Help us be faithful in our following of you in all the days of our lives. Help us be faithful until the end of our lives. And help all your people be faithful until the end of the age.

Amen.

CPSIA information can be obtained
at www.ICGtesting.com
Printed in the USA
LVHW080357030821
694377LV00014B/834